MANKYNDE IN SHAKESPEARE

MANKYNDE
IN SHAKESPEARE

Edmund Creeth

Athens
THE UNIVERSITY OF GEORGIA PRESS

Library of Congress Catalog Card Number: 74–15204
International Standard Book Number: 0–8203–0373–9
The University of Georgia Press, Athens 30602

© 1976 by the University of Georgia Press
All rights reserved

Set in 11 on 13 pt. Intertype Garamond
Printed in the United States of America

FOR LYN

—there, where I have garnered up my heart

Contents

Note of Gratitude

For help and encouragement over many years of thinking about this book, I especially thank Bertrand Evans, Robert S. Davis, Jocelyn Agnew Camp, Russell Fraser, Richard Barlow, and George Core.

E. C.

Textual Note

The nature of my argument forbids any thoroughgoing modernization of the many passages cited from medieval literature and from Shakespeare and his contemporaries. In my citations—chiefly from Mark Eccles' edition of the Macro plays for the E E T S and from the Shakespeare Folio—I have however printed *i, j, u* and *v* according to modern usage and replaced archaic symbols from the early texts by their equivalents: *th, y, gh.*

CHAPTER I

The Design
of the Protagonist's Experience

With the turn of the fifteenth century, in the period when the English mystery cycles reached their prime, there begin to appear in our records a few religious plays which are allegorical and theological rather than biblical, and which devote themselves—not to the history of the human race under God—but to the experience of the representative human individual between forces of good and evil contending for his soul. The oldest of these, written down about 1400 in blank spaces of a Latin account roll in Dublin, staged the initial rashness of the proud King of Life, his illuminating and chastening struggle with Death in the middle phase of the action, and, after his body is in the grave, the taking up of his soul from the brink of Hell through the intercession of Our Lady. James Mills of the Dublin Record Office, who discovered the play and published it in 1891, named it *The Pride of Life*.[1] Of these theological dramas about a universally representative central figure, there survive only three others that we may be certain are indigenous to England—all three as it happens calling him "Mankynde," all dramatizing not simply his moment of truth at the coming of death but the more discursive experiences of his temptation, and all surviving in a single collection of manuscripts put together by the eighteenth-century antiquarian Cox Macro. These were edited by F. J. Furnivall and published, for the first time conjointly and in their entirety, in 1904 as *The Macro Plays*.[2]

The best and most primitive of these (written about 1405) Furnivall entitled, not very helpfully, *The Castell of Perseverance*. The one truly "full scope" play that we possess, it sets out to imitate the whole spiritual life: Mankynde's baptismal innocence as he enters this world, his temptation by his own Evil Angel and the treacherous World, his enthronement as a king amid the Seven

Deadly Sins, his moral awakening at the touch of Penitencia's lance, the martial victory of his virtues over the sins in a siege of the Castle of virtuous middle age, his deception by the blandishments of the World and Coveytyse, his tyrannous old age and bitter death, the gratuitous rescue of his soul after intercession by Mercy and Peace, daughters of God. The second of the Macro plays (dated about 1460) Furnivall named, again misleadingly, *A Morality of Wisdom Who is Christ.* The playwright of *Wisdom* abandons the sprawling full scope idea in favor of a compact design in which Mankynde's grace, temptation—this time by the sophistry of a single tempter, Lucifer—sin, awakening, and restoration to grace are conceived of as phases of experience during a crucial period in his mature life. A member of the school of northern English mysticism founded by Rolle and Hilton, the dramatist thinks of mature virtue not in the military, psychomachian terms of the *Castell* playwright but in terms of love between Mankynde, or the parts of his soul analytically represented, and Christ-Wisdom. The third Macro play, composed as we have it perhaps in 1471, is *Mankind*, in roughly the same form as *Wisdom* but transmuting Mankynde into an English farmer. It is less deeply theological, lacking alike the rich religious symbolism of *Wisdom* and the moral sweep and grandeur of the *Castell* play, and though interpretations of it differ *Mankind* seems very close to parody. It was acted by a commercial troupe of players, evidently in Cambridgeshire.

Thus the plays of this kind whose auspices are those of faith rather than of profit, whose motive is to imitate man's life in the Christian scheme of things, his Godlike capability and the mystery of his iniquity, are the three oldest to survive: *The Pride of Life, The Castell of Perseverance,* and *Wisdom Who is Christ.* Each anonymous playwright achieves this mimesis in his own necessarily limited terms guided by universal Christian principles in one of two broad forms, that of the coming of death:

> Initial Vanity and Folly
> Agon and Recognition
> Salvation in Death

or that of the temptation play:

> Initial Innocence or Virtue
> Temptation
> Sin
> Recognition and Redemption.

In the former, the role of evil is not to tempt but to prove utterly false in the protagonist's time of need, the agon. The temptation pattern is doubled in the *Castell* play, beginning once with Mankynde's baptismal innocence and again with the established virtue of his fortieth year, ending first in moral awakening midway in the journey of his life and again, at death, in tragic recognition of the falseness of this world. Here, as in *The Pride of Life*, the tragedy is annulled by an Aeschylean resolution in Heaven. *Wisdom* incorporates the temptation plot in its single form as outlined, Mankynde reenacting it during a period of his adulthood touching directly neither birth nor old age and death.

The three plays share a common meaning stated in the last lines of *The Castell of Perseverance*, "Evyr at the begynnynge / Thynke on youre last endynge!" But they are not "moral plays" or "moralities"—names attached to them by eighteenth-century and later scholarship—in the narrowly didactic sense of having some "moral."[3] They are not, like the several Tudor interludes that copy their shape or like the French *moralités*, dramatic guides to some particular form of conduct, though each of them contains a measure of social criticism or social satire. The dénouements of *The Pride of Life* and the *Castell* play, in which the hero perceives the true nature of his folly in death or after death and is yet redeemed, are as amoral as moral. As Truth herself remarks after Mankynde's death,

> Late repentaunce if man save scholde,
>   Wheythyr he wrouth wel or wyckydnesse,
> Thanne every man wold be bolde
>   To trespas in trost of foryevenesse.
>   (ll. 3275–78)

And yet Mankynde is forgiven. No, the purpose of these dramas is not primarily to sermonize any more than it is primarily to entertain.[4] The early Tudor moral play is that which teaches a simple lesson in conduct. The aim here is rather to dramatize for the medieval audience gathered round the play the place and role of each of them in the Christian universe. "The case of our comynge you to declare," cried one of the flagbearers sent out a week in advance to advertise the performance of the *Castell* play in any given Norfolk or Lincoln-shire town, "Every man in hymself forsothe he it may fynde" (ll. 14–15). The two flagbearers do not call the play they summarize a "moral" nor give it any other designation. They speak of it as if it were simply *the* play, as in a sense it is or at least tries to be, and its power derives from the identification of each one of the assembled townspeople with Mankynde in his dual potential for Heaven or for Hell.

With these three plays—oldest, most serious in purpose, most nearly universal in scope of the native theological dramas of Mankynde's life—three Shakespearean tragedies exhibit the intimate, unique, and I think hitherto undiscovered kinship which it is my chief purpose in this book to define and try to understand. *The Castell of Persever-ance*, for example, when regarded in a Shakespearean perspective begins to bristle with uncanny intimations of *Macbeth*. These come to a head late in the play when Mundus, the world, turns to the Garcio who has been with him since with fair words and foul intent he first drew Mankynde from grace, dressed him in royal robes emblematic of the state of sin, and thus kept his promise that any man who serves and trusts him "schal be kynge." "How, boy, aryse!" cries the World. "Go brewe Mankynd a byttyr bende." Now Man-kynde must face the strange Boy, "a lyther lad with a torn hod" as we are told, who speaks with cruel sarcasm: "Whou faryst, Man-kynde, art thou ded?" He tugs at Mankynde's fallen body and confides to the audience that he wishes Mankynde were graved under the green. But Mankynde does not understand. "Abyde," he im-portunes the lad, raising himself to speak,

> What art thou? what woldyst thou mene?
> Wheydyr comyst thou for good or qwed?

> Wyth peynys prycke thou doste me tene,
>   The sothe for to sey.
> Telle me now, so God the save,
> Fro whom comyst thou, good knave?
> What dost thou here? what woldyst thou have?
>   Telle me or I deye.   (ll. 2926–33)

In essential conception and meaning, this moment brings us to the threshold of the scene not to be written for two hundred years in which Macbeth, only half comprehending, faces the bloody Child and the crowned Child. Like the procession of kings which follows, the Child is the symbol of the bitter future that Macbeth cannot prevent, wherein the seed of Banquo shall be kings, no son of his succeeding. The Garcio stands for the strangers "not of my blod," as Mankynde at last understands, who shall inherit his gold, holt and halls, and castle. All this, "the Werldys joye and hys jentyl jeste," the Boy explains, "Is now thyne, now myne." His name is itself a jest, couched in allegory: "My name is I Wot Nevere Whoo." Soon Mankynde is able to quote for the audience the scriptural inspiration of the scene: "ignorat cui congregabit ea." For this, like Macbeth, he has given his soul to Satanas, the common enemy of man. Within sight of the congregation stands Mankynde's personal devil, Malus Angelus, whom Mankynde like Macbeth (in Macduff's phrase) "still hath serv'd." The Boy, tattered and yet masterful, furthers a recognition on Mankynde's part that we may call tragic. Mankynde has already been struck, at the height of tyranny, by nemesis in the person of Death and has given eloquent expression to his resulting sense of spiritual desolation: "A, Deth, Deth! drye is thy dryfte. / Ded is my desteny" (ll. 2843–44). He has begun to grasp the treachery of this World. But he has still supposed, until now, that at least his costly acquisitions would go "to myne chyldyr and to myn wife." It is not to be so, "But a gedelynge I Wot Nevere Who / Hath al that the Werld me behyth" (ll. 2980–81).

In the system of equivalences which we may draw between the moral play and the tragedy, the Garcio suggests not only Banquo's nameless children who shall rule Scotland but all the hostile children on the stage and in the imagery whom Macbeth opposes but who triumph. Similarly, the deceiving World and his henchmen function like the Weird Sisters; the emblematic royal robes placed on Mankynde become both the actual robes in which Macbeth is invested king of Scotland and the ill-fitting clothing in the imagery. More centrally, the role of Mankynde in its spiritual outlines is reenacted by Macbeth.

Such equivalences indicate a rich and deep dramaturgic inheritance to be explored. But however much it may disclose of Shakespeare's roots in allegorical religious drama and may direct our attention toward overtones of meaning in such a play as *Macbeth*, it turns out, though truly rich and deep, to be unexpectedly limited and surprisingly discrete in extent. If *Macbeth* corresponds both in outline and in significant detail to one of the theological dramas about Mankynde, the same may be said of only the two other of Shakespeare's plays already designated. The three tragedies in question seem to have been contiguous in time of composition. *Othello* (ca. 1604) evidently inaugurates Shakespeare's career as a Jacobean tragic dramatist— however less "Jacobean" in spirit it may strike us than *Hamlet*, that brilliant and philosophical study in revenge and baffled idealism written two or three years back in a form created not by theological playwrights but by Seneca and Thomas Kyd. *King Lear* and *Macbeth* are claimed by scholarship for the years 1605–1606, although the order in which they were written remains doubtful. In the intimacy of their relationship to the old moral drama of England these three tragedies of Shakespeare are unique—not only among the plays of Shakespeare but against the extant work of his contemporaries, Elizabethan and Jacobean, as well. They alone shape themselves according to one of the two designs for Mankynde's experience, the temptation plot and the coming of death. They alone, therefore, since they are tragic avatars, move toward tragic recognition on the part of each protagonist of the folly of his chosen way of life. But the relationship is specific in yet another respect, for it turns out to be not simply a question of the generic resemblance of these tragedies to moral dramas. Each, rather, aligns itself—as *Macbeth* with the

Castell play—with a particular theological drama, from among the oldest to survive, more closely than it does with any other English play. These alignments, play to play—

> *The Castell of Perseverance—Macbeth*
> *Wisdom Who is Christ—Othello*
> *The Pride of Life—King Lear*

—strike me as so interesting that I have ventured to organize three chapters according to them.

Fully to perceive them requires a new calculus, a new instrument and language—which in these comparative studies may be imperfectly developed—for comparing literary works that employ radically different modes of imitating human life. I do not wish to suggest that the Shakespearean tragedies are allegories, or that Iago is really the Devil, much less that Desdemona is what is called in critical parlance a Christ-figure. It is more precisely that Iago as a character representing a man or demi-man plays a role, as sometimes the Vice does in Tudor drama, that was originally the Devil's, that Desdemona's part was first played by the character Wisdom who is indeed a Christ-figure. It fell to several figures in Tudor drama before it fell to her, none of them Christ though they share certain qualities of Christ: Bale's whitewashed and saintly Kyng Johan, for example, who is first to die in the role, Assuerus' wife godly Queen Hester, and most Desdemona-like perhaps, the jealous Count Walter's wife patient Grissell. The allegorical meaning that is the core meaning in the religious play may become figurative and peripheral, cast out as overtones of meaning in Shakespeare. It is so with Iago. To put it another way, what is metaphorical in Shakespeare, for example in Lear's vision of Hell and his salvation through the help of a "Soule in blisse," can be found enacted literally in the religious drama. Again, what is deliberately metaphorical in the old play (Christ represented as the wife and spouse of the Soul) may become quite literal in Shakespeare.

To grant this discrete Shakespearean atavism to be real one must approve the unconventional technique of comparing the allegorical with the literal modes of imitation that I have described and illustrated. Scholars of the subject may also have to free themselves from certain definitions and classifications which I have come to think are limiting and barren as well as from the evolutionist slant of nearly all studies of the pre-Shakespearean drama in its bearing upon Shakespeare and his contemporaries.[5] Hardin Craig, eminent authority both on Shakespeare and on religious drama, asks the key question— "Did the universally representative character, the fundamental feature of English moralities, live on into Tudor and Stuart drama?"—but gives a dusty answer because he is schooled in the ideas that drama necessarily evolves from recently preceding forms and that allegorical technique and not the design of the hero's experience is after all what is fundamental to what scholarship has chosen to call the English moralities.[6] Going on to a paragraph that shows *Macbeth* to be in perfect ethical harmony with the Macro plays, Craig yet remarks: "There is only the faintest possibility that there was any tangible influence of the moral interlude on Shakespeare when he wrote *Macbeth.* Certainly there are no obvious traces of the form as there are in the cases of Marlowe's *Doctor Faustus,* Dekker's *Old Fortunatus, A Merry Knack to Know a Knave,* and other Elizabethan plays."[7] These references show that by "obvious traces" Craig means archaisms.

A more adequate conception of influence reveals that a form of the primitive moral drama itself, more fully than the Tudor moral interlude, lives anew in *Macbeth.* It achieves this apotheosis by informing materials from Holinshed and accommodating the conventions of Jacobean tragedy. To acknowledge this thoroughgoing formal equivalence, only implicit and partial in the hybrid interlude, is to gain a perspective in which the kind of evidence already cited in relation to the *Castell* play and *Macbeth* makes itself available in profusion. Once perceived, it is as tangible and obvious as the outward trappings of allegorical drama in *Doctor Faustus,* though to be sure *Doctor Faustus* owes more to recent, Elizabethan permutations of moral drama than does *Macbeth.* The relationship of the Tudor interludes to Shakespeare's two tragedies of temptation is not a matter of gradual development in the Shakespearean direction but of Shakespeare's sudden and brilliant resolution midway in his career of the problem unresolved by Tudor playwrights of how to make literary tragedy out of the idea of the temptation plays like *The Castell of Perseverance* and *Wisdom Who is Christ.*

These relationships have remained to be discovered not because they are remote but because scholars of the subject are conditioned by evolutionist preconceptions. The stultifying traditional notions about what eighteenth-century and Victorian scholars dubbed ".the morality play" have further concealed them. I have given primacy to description of the relationships, to the tangible phenomena disclosed by my morphological approach, taking a cue from science lest these be obscured or seemingly invalidated by any unsatisfying effort to account for them. Literary scholarship might often gain, I think, by letting explanation wait upon observation and description. Why Shakespeare, and he alone, returned to the forms of native theological drama, and why this Shakespearean atavism belongs so discretely to 1604–1606, cannot, ultimately, be known. The last pages of this book set forth one man's effort at understanding it, but others it may be who grant its reality can better elucidate it than I out of their own vision of Shakespeare and the English Renaissance.

As for the other question *how*, manifestly what did happen could happen. I do not think that Shakespeare read manuscripts of plays in Middle English. He must have witnessed performances—perhaps at the dramatic center of Coventry near Stratford-upon-Avon—of dramas sufficiently like those preserved in our MSS. E. K. Chambers supposes that "moralities may have continued in out-of-the-way places to hold the open air stage, just as miracle plays did, to a comparatively late date."[8] Judging from vestiges preserved in the 1616 text of *Faustus*, Marlowe knew the theological temptation play though he did not finally choose to imitate it. W. Wager, as the discussion at the end of Chapter II will show, knew the *Castell* play or something closely related to it in early Elizabethan times. No one knows how. There are no records at all of any performances of the extant theological dramas although they certainly were performed. This is probably because these plays, unlike the mystery plays contemporary with them, were not matters for civic records.

As for Shakespeare, it could of course be argued that in transcending the interludes of temptation like *Apius and Virginia* and *Pacient Grissell* he by mere accident, or by a fresh infusion of Christian purpose, approximates the form of religious drama that lies behind these interludes. Conceivably so. But it is specifically and so it would seem deliberately in three consecutive tragedies that Shakespeare reiterates the patterns of archetypal English moral drama. He does so not only in the role of the tragic hero but in very numerous attendant details involved in the moral meaning of the role. At the same time, the methods of comparison suggested here yield nothing at all when applied to his other plays. The cumulative weight of these correspondences in three closely contemporary tragedies would seem to put the matter beyond the possibility of accident. It is the best proof that Shakespeare knew the archetypes intimately in some version.

What is more remarkable is the set of correspondences between *King Lear*, *Macbeth*, and *Othello* and precisely the three oldest English moral dramas extant today. The preservation of texts of these was rare good fortune. Two scribes spelled each other at copying *The Pride of Life* in unused spaces of the Latin account roll in Dublin, where it was discovered at the end of the last century. The vicissitudes of the Macro MSS were even more precarious, though a fragment of one of the plays, *Wisdom*, appears in the Digby collection. Presumably a large number of fifteenth-century moral dramas are lost along with the Paternoster plays. Did Shakespeare see in performance plays which fragile parchment alone kept in existence until they were printed around the turn of the twentieth century? Far more likely *The Pride of Life*, the *Castell* play, and *Wisdom* are representative of theological drama before the advent of commercial theater, or represent *states* of plays widely performed though varying somewhat according to time and place. There are reasons for thinking so. For example, the plot of the *Castell* play does not agree always with the summary of it in the Proclamation and hence must not have been always the same. Clearly the extant plays were not isolated. The *Castell* drama as we have it evidently toured Lincolnshire and Norfolk but in one version or another deeply influenced the Digby play of *Mary Magdalene* from another region. Philological evidence shows *Wisdom* to have been composed in a northerly dialect, yet both its manuscripts, except for rhyme words, are in the dialect of London. The play must then have traveled extensively, although no more so than *The Pride of Life*, which Brandl thinks was composed in the south but which exists in northern dialect in the Dublin manuscript. The recurrent temptation patterns in the Tudor interludes examined below are sufficient to imply that *Wisdom* and the *Castell* play typify their native progenitors. In short, Plantagenet moral drama may have been more homogeneous than has been thought. *The Castell of Perseverance*, *Wisdom*, and *The Pride of Life* may embrace its chief varieties and stand fairly for the whole. At any rate, such an hypothesis helps explain the underlying correspondences between Plantagenet theological dramas of Mankynde and three Shakespearean tragedies.

CHAPTER II

Count Walter and the Worldly Man

Tudor playwrights in their concern with the more immediate benefits of virtuous living seem seldom or never to have patterned their own plays after the inherently eschatological design shared by *The Pride of Life* and *Everyman*. We may set aside *Everyman*, perhaps of Dutch origin and perhaps unperformed, however widely read, in Tudor England, and a play or pantomime called *The Cradle of Security*, which survives only in an account of an early Elizabethan performance and seems in any case to have lacked the phase of spiritual salvation.[1] Otherwise there exists between *The Pride of Life* and *King Lear* no play modeled on the coming of death.

But the alternative design of temptation, the design developed so far as our records show in the three Macro plays, lent itself readily to the expression of new themes and ideas on the Tudor stage. Design, the pattern of the experience of the protagonist, not allegory or the use of personified abstractions as characters, is the general criterion for distinguishing the relevant Tudor interludes. Thus the play of *Godly Queene Hester* is in the line connecting *Wisdom* and *Othello* because the biblical story has been reshaped to make of Assuerus a Mankynde-figure. *Hester* is not only based on the Bible but much affected by the Tudor penchant for making drama out of debate. Other biblical interludes contemporary with it—Bale's *Chefe Promyses of God*, *Johan Baptystes Preachynge in the Wyldernesse*, and *The Temptacyon of Our Lorde*, and the anonymous *Johan the Evangelyst*, though like *Hester* it mingles abstractions with biblical figures—in contrast do not at all perpetuate the design of Mankynde's virtue, temptation, sin, and regenerative realization. Other interludes indebted to the debate—Heywood's early plays *Wytty and Wyttles*, *Love*, and *Wether*, the *Gentylnes and Nobylyte* attributed to John

Rastell—like Medwall's *Fulgens* bear not the slightest impress of Mankynde's experience. Heywood's later plays *The Pardoner and the Frere, The Foure P. P.*, and *Johan Johan the Husbande* take form from Chaucer and French farce, not from anything resembling the Macro plays. *Nice Wanton*, though certainly a morality play, is rooted like the early Elizabethan *Disobedient Child* in Continental humanistic school drama and so exhibits nothing of the temptation plot. Bale's *Thre Lawes, of Nature, Moses, and Christ*, though also indubitably moral drama, is shaped according to an original, not the traditional, structural pattern. But Bale's remaining extant play, *Kyng Johan*, is in the Macro tradition because Nobilyte–Clergye–Civil Order move through Mankynde's pattern of experience in relation to Johan just as Mynde-Wyll-Understanding had done in relation to the regal Wisdom in *Wisdom Who is Christ*. The three rogues in *Hyckescorner*, Frewyll, Imagination, and Hyckescorner, have been said to be related to the triple protagonist of *Wisdom*, but if they are, the pattern, and the effect, of their experience is quite different. The writing is competent, the intent serious, the doctrine Catholic, but in making up his own plot out of older elements the dramatist loses the hold upon his audience that might have come from their universal identification with a protagonist. The title figure in the *Enterlude of Youth*, in which all the characters are abstractions, is reprobate from the start, never innocent and never tempted, though he is improved in the fashion of the temptation tradition by moral awakening and penance at the close. Yet the hero of *Lusty Juventus*, R. Wever's anti-Catholic youth play curiously allied in spirit to Redford's *Wyt and Science*, retains all the phases of the temptation plot except for a slight modification at the start. This, the most common variant in the Tudor reenactments of the plot, is that the Mankynde-figure, now Calvinistically "of nature, prone to vice" although "by grace and good counsayll, trayneable to vertue" as Wever's title page phrases it, must be trained to virtue from a state of moral frailty before temptation and sin can occur.

Grace and virtue, temptation, sin, realization, and penance undergo all sorts of translations out of the theological into political, economic, polemic, educational, and other secular realms as a series of protag-

onists reenact Mankynde's pattern of experience. Especially when
the design informs and reshapes for the stage materials from fiction,
the Bible, or English history, these sequential phases of experience
are likely to take on new immediacy, particularity, and concreteness.
This survival of the temptation plot in various secular incarnations
supplies a line of demonstrable continuity from Lancastrian moral
drama that runs through allegorical, hybrid, and in at least one
instance wholly literal drama, figures equally in the so-called popular
tradition and theater of a coterie, and culminates in a few early
Elizabethan attempts to write tragedy of temptation. A knowledge
of the full scope or doubled plot and, more important, of Mankynde's
single encounter with temptation as evolved in *Wisdom*, provides the
best instrument for studying the participation of the moral play in
Tudor drama and, often, for studying the dramaturgy of an individual playwright. It was not so much, we discover, that the
theological drama "contributed abstractions" as that it contributed
design, a way to make a play embodying a system of ideas and to
adapt a story for the stage. Roughly half of the extant Tudor plays
composed between 1498 and 1558 are moral interludes in this
sense—that they perpetuate the structure of the theological temptation
plays of the fifteenth century to teach virtuous conduct. It is as if for
one class of playwrights Mankynde's pattern was simply *the* pattern
for the protagonist of a play.

   Some fifteen interludes are thus distinguished from the others
which, with the notable exception of the work of John Heywood,
are as a rule also didactic but take their structure from the story used
as a source, from Continental dramatic models, or from debate, or
employ an original structure. The bent of the temptation plays is
tragic, even though the plot occasionally yields pure comedy and
though all the exemplars up until Elizabethan times end happily for
their Mankynde-figure, restored to grace, favor, or prosperity by
the salutary consequences of his recognition of the moral truth as
that truth has been established by the dramatist. The interludes in
question, that is, though occasionally light, witty, trivial, deal on the
whole with human conflict such as leads to suffering and bodes
catastrophe as its resolution. This is very true of as early a specimen

as Skelton's *Magnyfycence* (ca. 1516). In Bale's *Kyng Johan*, written according to the playwright in 1538 but revised for Elizabeth, the title figure, whose role is that of Christ-Wisdom in the Macro play, dies wretchedly, though the central figures, a composite protagonist as in *Wisdom*, endure a bitter realization of their folly and thereby end in political bliss. We might expect the native play of temptation, now secularized and congenial to literary materials, to participate strongly in the birth of English stage tragedy which takes place almost at once upon the accession of Elizabeth. But there are reasons why it cannot do so. Actually, the influence of the temptation plot is discernible in only seven Elizabethan plays, all of them composed early in the new era from 1559 to about 1572, and even in these it does not survive without severe distortion.[2]

The chief cause, the new pressure of crudely tragic purpose, is best seen by considering the scene of realization of religious or ethical truth which before 1558 always ended the phase of sin and initiated spiritual regeneration. Delusion, that is, required and supplied the potential for moral awakening. A significant stage direction marking the point at which in Skelton's play Magnyfycence's mind begins to grasp the truth reads, "*Here goth* Foly *away.*" "Why," exclaims the king to Fansy in nascent realization, "who wolde have thought in you such gyle!" He learns the real name of his chief deceiver Cloked Colusyon and the extent of his own misconduct. "Alasse my Foly! alasse my wanton Wyll," he weeps.[3] After adversity and despair, he regains integrity, and solvency, through penance and the grace of God. Redresse clothes him appropriately.

Such a scene of realization occurs regularly in the work of other Tudor moral dramatists until about 1558, and always at the same point in the design—after depiction of initial innocence or virtue, temptation, and sinful folly. It is stirred in a variety of ways. The second recognition scene in John Redford's *Wyt and Science* illustrates particularly well the ability inherent in this part of the plot to survive in new contexts.[4] In the oldest enactment of the scene in English drama, Confescio had told Mankynde of the *Castell* play, "Behold thynne hert, . . . And thynne owyn consyense" and, Penitencia having made him contrite, regenerated him through an enactment of the sacrament of penance. The playwright of *Wisdom* had dramatized the scene of the "recognycion ye have clere" by the symbolic use of vesture characteristic of him. Mynde and the other faculties of Mankynde are made to look with astonishment upon the image of Anima their soul, really their own image, that now appears in the "most horrybull wyse, fowlere than a fende" as the result of their misdeeds. As contrition floods over them, Anima is soon able to say, "I begyn awake, / I that this longe hath slumberyde in syne." The composite protagonist leaves the stage to be reformed by the sacrament of penance and soon returns, the parts of the soul "all in here fyrst clothynge." Wyt's astonished perception of his true appearance in his glass of Reason is Redford's ingenious adaptation of the kind of confrontation with self that we find in *Wisdom*. At first, still unregenerate, Wyt in fact supposes that he sees a fiend's image reflected in the mirror: "Hah! Goges sowle! What have we here? A dyvyll? / This glas, I se well, hath bene kept evyll" (ll. 802–3). Rubbing the glass and peering into it again, Wyt perceives himself more clearly: "Goges sowle! a foole! a foole, by the mas" (l. 828). Testing the glass by holding it up to the bright faces in the audience, Wyt at last realizes that he has indeed been made a fool, equipped with the coat, hood, ears, and cockscomb of Ignoraunce. "And as for this face," he adds (ll. 815–16), "[it] is abhominable, / As black as the devyll!" He acknowledges that the change in him is the work of Idleness, that Science rightly disdained him, and that instead of the four gifts of the World he has won hatred, beggary, and open shame. Reason himself now returns, bringing Shame, who beats the culprit while instead of Christian confession Reason reads off a list of his humanistic sins: that he broke his promise to marry Science and obey Instruccion, set his love upon Idleness, let her make a fool of him, and offended God and man by swearing oaths as great as a man can. The episode recalls the coming of Shamefastness and Reason to Mankynde in Medwall's temptation play *Nature*, but it reaches farther back to the scenes of contrition and confession in the Macro plays. Wyt, like Mankynde in *Wisdom*, is to be perfected in his regeneration and trimmed in new apparel offstage, but by

Instruccion, not Holy Church. The parallel is complete even to the awkwardness of both Wisdom's and Reason's having to think of something to say to fill up the time required by the hero's change of costume. His face washed and clothing restored (the oaths having vanished from his vocabulary during the long speech of recognition), Wyt is fitted to slay Tediousness with his sword of comfort, climb Parnassus to his bride Science, and enter into his heaven upon earth.

Even though *Wyt and Science* is children's drama and humanist comedy, not tragedy, it shows how Tudor interludes may both derive from Lancastrian moral drama and anticipate the great tragic art of *Othello*. The release of passion in Wyt's second phase of "sin," his concomitant threat to strike his beloved or do worse to her, the related degeneration of his speech, the painful, regenerative return of self-knowledge and reason—all have their parallels, with essentially similar meaning, in *Othello*. Further, as in *Wisdom*, black is the emblem of the irrational, the "abhominable" and devilish, and the blackness of Wyt's smudged face anticipates the sinfulness that Othello finds "as black as mine own face" and the deed that makes him appear to Emilia "the blacker Divell." So does Wyt's comic cry of self-discovery, "a foole! a foole, by the mas," prefigure Othello's tragic exclamation, "O Foole, foole, foole!"

In Medwall's *Interlude of Nature* (written about 1498) Reason himself admonishes and awakes the hero, Mankynde.[5] Good Counsel, revealing the trickery of the Devil, that author of lies, performs similar service for Lusty Juventus, who falls to the ground and exclaims, "Alas, alas, what have I wrought and done? . . . / Thus in my first age to worke myne own destruction."[6] In Scotland, the design figures in the career of Sir David Lyndsay's King Humanity, to whom Divine Correction cries, "Get up, sir King! ye haif sleipit aneuch / Into the armis of Ladie Sensual," and to whom Verity explains that villainy "did begyle your Excellence." Remarking "I se they have playit me the glaiks," he asks instruction of Good Counsel and receives it together with a promise that if it is heeded his fame and name shall be perpetual.[7] Among protagonists who are concrete individuals, Melebea, persuaded by the bawd Celestina in the role of Sensuality that surrendering herself to Calisto would be Christian

charity rather than sin, is stirred to moral awakening not by Good
Counsel but by her good father Danio. "All pensyfe and sore
abasshyd" after hearing his words of admonition, she declares, "Alas
dere fader, alas, what have I done? / Offendyd god as a wrech
unworthy."[8] (This recognition scene, a contribution of the English
dramatic tradition, is of course wholly independent of *La Celestina*,
the playwright's literary source.) To the heroine of Lewis Wager's
Edwardian morality play *Marie Magdalene* comes the personified
abstraction Knowledge of Sinne.[9] King Assuerus, to cite finally the
temptation play drawing its material from the Book of Esther, learns
the true merit of the Jews whom he had been led to persecute, his
unwitting threat to the life of his godly wife, and the true character
of the calumniator Aman. To this tempter he exclaims in words
reminiscent of Magnyfycence at the same point in the design,

> O kaytiffe most crafty o false dissembler,
> With thy flattering tonge thou haste deceyved me,
> All noble princes by me may be ware
> Whom they shall truste and put in auctorite.[10]

Such realization of folly enables each of these protagonists to regain
the particular state of virtue proper to him, as a rule defined upon his
first appearance.

But this seemingly indispensable phase of the didactic plot, the
scene of realization, is abruptly blotted out when the moral interludes,
after 1558, begin to carry tragic meaning and, more often than not,
to end in catastrophe for the erring central figure. The primary
reason is probably not far to seek. How should moral awakening,
serving hitherto to fit the Lancastrian or early Tudor protagonist
for his return to grace or to virtuous discipline, be retained in face of
a just reward for secular misdeeds committed in the state of sin?
John Phillip's *Pacient and Meeke Grissell* and W. Wager's *Inough
is as Good as a Feast*, alike composed in the nascent period of English
tragedy, typify the failure of the moral tragedies, all belonging to
this period, to realize the potential, inherent in the temptation plot,
to yield a powerful closing scene of tragic recognition, of punishment
according to worldly justice of a hero restored to nobility through

awareness of his folly. Still, in our Shakespearean perspective, it is remarkable that one playwright applied the plot to the story of a husband tempted to distrust his innocent wife, and another used it to dramatize the consequences, under God, of tyrannous ambition on the part of a flawed and deluded magistrate.

No Tudor play is so pervasively akin to *Othello* as is the theological drama *Wisdom*, nor would *Pacient Grissell* be, even if Phillip had carried through to a recognition scene on the part of his protagonist. It is not a question of dramatic evolution toward *Othello*. Nonetheless, the intermediate plays frequently show the potential for something like *Othello* in the idea of the temptation plot in its compact form first witnessed in *Wisdom*. There Mankynde, deluded by the Devil, does wrong to a character embodying goodness. In fact Wisdom, as we have noted, is conceived to be figuratively man's spouse, and grace is marriage to Wisdom, who is Christ. At certain moments the accents of the figurative bride suggest how the role might someday fall to Desdemona:

> What have I do? why lowyste thou not me?
>   Why cherysyste thi enmye? Why hatyst thou thi frende?
> Myght I have don ony more for the?
>   But love may brynge drede to mynde.
>   (ll. 913–16)

In Tudor drama, the traditional temptation plot with its triangle of parts for evil, good, and free-willed protagonist occasionally invades literary sources dealing with a man's relationship to a woman. The embodiment of goodness in the hero's life first becomes his wife in the interlude that makes a Tudor political allegory out of the Book of Esther. The unknown author of *Godly Queene Hester* is also among the first to assign Mankynde's role, as outlined earlier, to a concrete individual taken from a literary source.

The possibility that the design could inform literal drama is clear even in *Mankind* (ca. 1475), the third of the Macro plays.[11] Unlike its two predecessors and several Tudor successors, *Mankind* is not fundamentally, but only nominally, allegorical. Its protagonist is a typical farmer, Mankynde only in name and in the pattern of his experience. Titivillus, the tempter, is not quite human, but not quite the Devil either,[12] and Mercy, the representative of spiritual goodness, is neither Christ nor, despite his name, a personified abstraction but Mankynde's "father gostly" (l. 764) and the "goode man Mercy" (l. 527), a priest, the channel by which divine mercy may reach Mankynde's soul. Thus the tempter's sophistry may for the first time take on the form of explicit slander. In the temptation scene (ll. 541–606), as Mankynde is momentarily offstage, Titivillus boasts as will Iago at the same stage of the plot of the change wrought in the protagonist. "Looke where he comes," says Iago to the audience as the protagonist returns, and Titivillus: "Mankynde cummyth ageyn, well fare he!" The hero, disillusioned with labor and prayer, falls into a sleep that is troubled by the whispering voice of Titivillus slandering Mercy:

> Alasse, Mankynde, alasse! Mercy stown a mere!
> He ys runn away fro hys master, ther wot no man where;
>   Moreover, he stale both a hors and a nete.
>
> But yet I herde sey he brake hys neke as he rode in Fraunce;
> But I thynke he rydyth on the galouse, to lern for to daunce,
>   Because of hys theft, that ys hys governance.
> Trust no more on hym, he ys a marryde man.
>   (ll. 594–600)

In Skelton's *Magnyfycence*, the protagonist's moral mainstay, without whom his life falls into disorder, is his friend Measure, and at the very outset he sagely puts Lyberte and Felycyte in Measure's keeping. Measure, like Wisdom and Mercy, like Desdemona in the life of Othello, is the thing that stands against spiritual chaos. "Measure and I," Magnyfycence declares (ll. 186–87), "wyll never be devyded, / For no dyscorde that any man can sawe." In his friend's temperance, he adds, "I have suche delight, / That Measure shall never departe from my syght." Measure's response suggests again that he is one of those figures in Tudor drama who stand midway between Christ-Wisdom and Desdemona:

> I trowe Good Fortune hath annexyd us together
> To se howe greable we are of one mynde;
> There is no flaterer nor losyll so lyther,
> This lynkyd chayne of love that can unbynde.
>
> (ll. 198–201)

The speech foreshadows, and is given retrospective irony by, the temptation. We rightly anticipate that slander will be directed against Measure, and that the prince's rejection of him will initiate the phase of sin.

In the *Hester* play the plot reasserts itself in materials drawn from Scripture so as to yield a human tempter, an individualized protagonist-husband, and for the first time a literal woman in the role of Christ-Wisdom. Mardocheus praises his foster child in words that anticipate Brabantio's description of the maiden never bold, Desdemona:

> a virgin puer,
> A pearle undefiled and of conscience cleare
> Sober, sad, jentill, meke and demure,
> In learninge and litterature, profoundely seene,
> In wisdome, eke semblante to Saba the Quene
> Fytt for any prince to have in marriage—
>
> (ll. 255–60)

His stress on her learning is justified by Hester's remarkable speech on the uses a king may have for his "Quenes wysdome," and Assuerus doubts not

> but the wysdome of us two
> Knytte both to gether in parfytte charyte
> All thynges in thys realme shall cumpas so,
> By truth and Justice, law and equitye,
> That we shall quenche all vice and deformite.
>
> (ll. 296–300)

Though it would be imprudent to attach much importance to the recurrence of the term "wysdome" and to the reference through

Mardocheus to Solomon and Sheba (Saba), this first phase in the experience of Assuerus (ll. 1–337) has a certain affinity to the opening scene of *Wisdom* in its ceremonial representation of love and a marriage as mainstays of the hero's virtue. The assemblage on stage departs in a procession that would resemble in performance the exeunt of the principals and the five virgins in white standing for the Wits at the close of the corresponding first phase of *Wisdom:* "Here departith the queene & Aman & all the maidens."

The playwright, though guided in part by the details of Henry's actual marriage, clearly has in mind the first requirement of the temptation plot as he seeks to establish Assuerus as a just monarch so that his later wrongdoing may be seen as the result of an insidious temptation. This opening scene is of course highly original in relationship to its scriptural source. Chapter 1 of Esther, with its wine-drinking and wrathful king, is unsuitable as a model in the instruction of a Christian magistrate.

In the temptation (ll. 605–774) Aman calumniates not Hester but the Jews—they have alien ceremonies and reject the laws and rule of the prince, supposing themselves exempt; they may occasion rebellion, and their substantial possessions make them dangerously powerful. Hence the king should give order

> To slea these Jewes in your realme over all,
> None to escape let your sentence be generall,
> Ye shall by that wynne to say I dare be bolde,
> To your treasure .x. thousande pound of golde.
>
> (ll. 754–57)

Mistaking his own cruelty and greed for justice, Assuerus soon consents to issue the order. It is not yet clear to him, nor perhaps to the dramatist himself, that the general sentence by implication includes his wife Hester.

Assuerus' folly is succinctly dramatized (ll. 775–868) by the introduction of four Jews (an obvious redeployment of actors who played the Gentlemen and the three vices) lamenting the king's unjust rigor and his credulity. One of the Jews is Hester's foster father, Mardocheus. She, overhearing these laments, is motivated like Penitencia, Wisdom, Mercy, or Reason in earlier plays to disabuse the protagonist. The chapel choir sings a holy hymn as if to gain divine support for her intention "To inspyre the prynce, & his mynd incence" so that the Jews may be saved. "Eke to dysclose the falsed favell and fraude / Of this cruell Aman . . ." (ll. 864–68).

Hester is permitted to play Christ-Wisdom opposite her husband's Mankynde. The tempter's slander has not touched her, or it has not occurred to Assuerus that it has, and before she has chided him he reminds us again of her perfections, "Of personage pearles and in wisdom alone," and he kisses her. She, though praising his "hye magnyficens," bounty, and grace, admonishes him, arguing the real hospitality of the Jews and exposing the character of their slanderer. For the first time the danger to Hester herself is made explicit. Unless he pardons them "I and all they by one condemnation, / To deathe are determined . . ." (ll. 916–17). Aman she describes as "oure mortall enymye" who out of cruel envy

> putteth other in blame
> Deludinge youre grace, when he lyst to fayne
> And no man so worthy for to suffer payne,
> As he him selfe that by hys poyson and gall,
> Hath deceyved you, and eke youre commons all.
> (ll. 938–42)

We have already noted Assuerus' realization of the moral truth. It enables him to conclude with exemplary acts of that justice he had espoused at the start, among them the sentencing of Aman to be hanged. But the Othello-like potential of the interlude is implicit in the king's letter read by a scribe after the action is completed:

> Had we not spyed his subtile behavoure
> He wolde have dystroyd quene Hester our wyfe
> And from us at the lengthe have taken our lyfe.
> (ll. 1135–37)

The last Tudor play in the line stemming from *Wisdom Who is Christ* is John Phillip's *Pacient and Meeke Grissell* (ca. 1558–1561).[13] Even despite his wretched fourteeners, Phillip by working

out to its logical end his fusion of the tale of Griselda with the traditional dramatic design would have produced a drama of some intrinsic
worth as a tragedy of human folly. Another Iago-like tempter, again
"honest," leads the individual inheritor of Mankynde's part to shatter
a marriage of true minds with acts of outrageous cruelty. The
motiveless Vice (whom Phillip must invent, finding no tempter in
his source) seeks "prively her confusion to worke." The saintly, in-
comprehending Grissell can but wonder "how is my Lord abused."
The husband Gautier, after the temptation scene, commits what we
are explicitly made to regard as "sinne against my love" (l. 1579).
Gautier, then, insofar as the play belongs structurally to the morality
tradition, is the protagonist, though much in the play justifies the
titular stress on the wife's patience, as in Petrarch and Chaucer. All
of Phillip's elaborate changes from the old tale to bring it into line
with other temptation plays lead us to anticipate a scene of Gautier's
realization of his folly in harkening to the whispering Vice. Instead,
Phillip drops the Vice out of the play after the temptation scene
and permits the marquis to wind things up in bland forgetfulness
that he has sinned against his love.

The whole purpose of the scenes between Politic Perswasion's
monologue of self-introduction and his assault upon Gautier's faith,
structurally considered, is to represent the union of Gautier and
Griselda as a marriage of true minds. That Gautier should be
accompanied upon his first entrance by Sansper (sans-peer) Fidence,
Reason, and Sobrietie is a fact of structural importance, not a mere
archaism of characterization. The play is "hybrid," to be sure. Phillip
does not manage to express these virtues of his protagonist entirely
through word and deed as Shakespeare would. Sobrietie is that part
of Gautier's mind which sees the need to marry. Reason and Peerless
Faith are precisely those qualities of Gautier's mind which Perswasion
will have to subvert in the temptation. The Vice, whom they have
chanced upon while hunting, mutters a cynical response to their
praises of the marquis and thus attracts his attention. He then comes
nearer to seeing the real nature of the Vice than he will later when
deceived by a name: "What art thou that thus unreverently dost
prate?" (l. 87), words which may remind students of Shakespeare of

Brabantio's similar "What prophane wretch art thou?" And when he gets the drift of the nobles' counsel, the Vice, lacking with Iago any grasp of true love, can only remark (1. 163), "Bones is all this intretaunce for wivinge?"

It is wiving Gautier has in mind, nor is he motivated by base carnality: "I am not Venus darlinge . . . / Hir bestiall playes I hate" (ll. 660–62). We are in a realm somewhere between the *Wisdom*-playwright's stress on reason over sensuality and Othello's insistence that he does not seek to please the palate of his sexual appetite. The lovers, to signify their mutual harmony, sing together a duet, of which these lines sung by Gautier will give some notion:

> Thy Vertues seem no lesse to bee
> With *Alcest* fayre compare you maye
> Thy modest life inflamed mee
> To joyne and knit this knot to daye. . . .
>
> (ll. 864–67)

The duet reminds one of the loving "tota pulcra es" at the close of the corresponding phase of *Wisdom*, a century earlier.

Between this moment of perfect union and that of Gautier's ordering of the persecutions (ll. 889–1005) Phillip puts the course of the action into the control of the Vice and it would seem decisively commits *Pacient Grissell* to the form of an English play of temptation. The characteristic language of Vices blends with an Iago-like two-faced pretence of "love" as Politic exposes himself in the monologue that a dramatist with more control and foresight might have used instead of Heywoodian foolery earlier in the play:

> This geare cannot chuse but breed inconvenience,
> I will not cease prively her confusion to worke,
> For under Honnie the proverbe saith poyson maye lurke:
> So though I simulate externally Love to pretend,
> My love shall turne to mischife, I warrant you in the end.
>
> (ll. 896–900)

Reason and Sobrietie, who enter praising Grissell, resist his "mallice," seeing it for what it is. In this temptation scene from hybrid drama,

Perswasion is partly trying to stir up rancor in two courtiers, partly contacting the reason and sobriety characteristic thus far of Gautier. News that Grissell has brought forth a child (Politic speculates in Iago's animalistic mode that it might rather have been a "Pigge" or a "litter," her belly was so big) gives the tempter leverage upon Gautier's mind (l. 961) "Wherwith I will molest and distroye her cleane." "Let me see even so . . ." he muses, as the protagonist enters in person, literally singing his wife's praises, then reaffirming to himself the divine providence manifest in the marriage, his absolute satisfaction, so that there may be (to borrow E. E. Stoll's phrase) steep tragic contrast to his attitude toward her under the Vice's influence. It is the loving rapture of Mankynde in *Wisdom*, of King Assuerus, and finally of Othello that outward honesty, inward infidelity, can so easily transform. For in a single speech the Vice creates poisonous distrust where there was until this moment perfect trust. If she is so virtuous as the marquis imports, remarks Perswasion,

> Shee may be made a saynte for her good conversacion:
> But harke my Lorde nay nowe harken in your eare,
> Try hir that waye and by myne honestie I sweare,
> You shall see hir decline from Vertues so rife
> And alter topsie turvie hir saintish lyfe:
> Hir pacyence quicklye shall chaunged bee,
> I warrant your honor will say it is not shee.
>
> (ll. 995–1001)

We are to understand that after line 996 the tempter whispers into the protagonist's ear, like the first of the calumniators believed in moral drama, the whispering Titivillus, a plan of action related to the slander: namely that the child be forcibly taken from Grissell to test her reaction. Like Mankynde before and Othello after him, Gautier ratifies diabolic suggestion as if it were sanctified: "As sure as God doth lyve, and sitt in heaven above, / So sure will I in every poynt, this thy device approve" (ll. 1002–3). This is the traditional moment of moral choice of the temptation plays.[14]

It is under the influence of "poyson" distilled by a malicious and hypocritical mind, then, that Gautier in Phillip's play performs his three traditional acts of cruelty. Politic hates Grissell, as Willard Farnham well says,[15] simply because she is good, and his aim, successfully achieved, is to bring about her confusion by controlling her husband. After the apparent slayings of her daughter and son, Politic takes the marquis aside and whispers into his ear the climactic folly, that Grissell be sent home as unworthy to be his wife. Here, as thus far throughout this section of the play, Gautier's passivity is frighteningly absolute: "Say what you please I am ready the to heare. . ." (l. 1490). She is willing to go if that will end the consuming agony which she fancies exists in her husband's mind because of the complaints of commons and nobility about her lowly lineage. Piteously, she requests only a smock to cover her, since it is unfitting that she should depart naked. When she is gone, the Vice tells us that he "will be packing" (l. 1669). He has exulted, in soliloquy, at the success of his "pollicies" since bringing about the first of the tests, and now with Grissell sent away in disgrace he clearly believes that he has accomplished his purpose, "prively her confusion to worke." The tempter of the English moral play, in this Tudor reembodiment as a Vice, has found his true element in the dramatization of the Griselda story, his traditional opportunity to win at least temporary victory over the saintly representative of good, variously played hitherto by Bonus Angelus, the Wisdom who is Christ, Mercy, Queen Hester or Kyng Johan, through deception of a wavering central figure, originally Mankynde. To dismiss Politic as merely the vestigial "buffoon of the old Moralities" is to fail to see the place of *Pacient Grissell* here at the dawn of the Elizabethan age in the main line of English drama up to this time.

The operation of the plot of the native moral play in *Pacient Grissell* up until the final exit of the Vice may be summarized as follows:

> Introduction of Evil Agency (ll. 1–55)
> Initial Virtue (ll. 56–888)
> Temptation (ll. 889–1005)
> Sin (ll. 1006–1670).

Both the tradition of the Lancastrian and Tudor moral plays and the inner logic of the piece lead us to expect *Pacient Grissell* to end with Gautier's moral realization and painful return to his original impressive stature. He should realize that he has acted the fool in listening to the counsel of Politic Perswasion, weep the medicinal tears of contrition, perhaps bring about punishment of the rascal who has done so much mischief, beg forgiveness of Grissell and, a sadder and wiser man, restore her. In leading up to and managing the temptation scene, Phillip has done some writing independently of his source with fair success, and what is required of him now seems no more than what Tudor playwrights had already achieved in conceiving new endings in the manner of the moral play for *La Celestina* and the Book of Esther. But Gautier is not to endure the salutary awakening of his many predecessors in Mankynde's role, for Phillip ends the play according to the old story of Griselda, just as if he had never varied from it.

Yet it would not have been such a simple matter as at first appears for Phillip to have ended with consistency and telling effect the temptation play that he began and then abandoned with the departure of the Vice. Before the divorce of Catherine of Aragon, a Tudor Griselda play, if anyone had dared write it, might easily, like *Godly Queene Hester*, have pointed the way of virtue to Henry VIII in a scene of realization and penitent reconciliation. But Phillip is not dealing at this point of his play with any political issue. No more is he expressing, through the pattern of his hero's experience, any straightforward lesson in proper conduct, like his incidental lessons in wifely constancy and filial obedience. What would be the meaning of Gautier's realization that he has already done harm for which he can never entirely atone, and for whom would a scene of such realization be intended? No early Elizabethan popular or court dramatist could be expected to preach the subtle lesson of Shakespeare and Keats in negative capability, the lesson that it may be wrong to strive for certainty in human relations. Nor could such a dramatist write a recognition scene with an eye to emotional effect, catharsis, the provocation of pity and fear. What his combination of dramatic and literary materials holds out to Phillip, in brief, is tragic recognition, and this is something for which no playwright or audience of his time was ready. One may even doubt whether Phillip himself wholly understands the new frame of deception in which he has placed the behavior of the Marquis of Salucia. At only one, early point in the phase of sin (l. 1196), is it explicit, when Grissell in five words touches unwittingly on the truth: "Alas my woe increaseth much, *how is my Lord abused.*" Instantly, she moves away from it: "Nay rather . . . ," Nature urges her to lament, "To see how cruell destinie, against me doth prevaile. . . ." Phillip himself finally wavers between the new theme brought in by the influence of moral drama, how Gautier is abused, and the old one, how Fortune is cruel to Griselda. If the design of moral drama has given his play the original stress of Boccaccio upon the bestial folly of the marquis, he ends by moralizing it in the manner of Petrarch as an example of patience in the face of worldly affliction rewarded at last. When the story is viewed in this light, it is as in Philippe de Mézières and Chaucer and in *L'estoire de Griseldis*, about the marquise, and her husband is only instrumental, the form taken by worldly or marital adversity in her life. It focuses upon the woman's humble acceptance and remarkable constancy as emblems of a Christian virtue. In this view, to condemn her husband's acts as foolish or criminal is irrelevant. But in Phillip's interlude these are patently caused by a malicious practice upon his credulity. The result is the absurd final complacency of Phillip's hero.

Within a year or two of the time when Phillip chanced to combine the temptation plot with Boccaccio's tale of the Marquis of Salucia mistrustful of his saintly wife, the even more obscure playwright W. Wager turned back to the *Castell* play or to something closely similar and refashioned it as an Elizabethan tragedy of sinful ambition. Worldly Man's experience leaves no doubt that he is Wager's version of Mankynde, more directly related than Gautier to the medieval archetype because no literary source has intervened in his conception. Picking up the theme of worldliness and tyranny of the *Castell* play rather than that of violated love introduced into moral drama through the more mystical religion of *Wisdom*, Wager's tragedy anticipates *Macbeth* just as *Pacient Grissell* anticipates *Othello*. Worldly Man, like Mankynde and Macbeth, cannot rest content with "inough," with the benefits he already enjoys as a virtuous and respected man. Solicited by agents of evil, he seeks more and more, in growing cruelty and growing wretchedness, believing that ruthless acquisition, while not good in itself, will be best for him within the bounds of this life.

Wager's play comes to us under an unpromising title: *A Comedy or Enterlude intituled, Inough is as Good as a feast, very fruteful, godly and ful of pleasant mirth.*[16] It is by far the most affecting of the seven early Elizabethan plays influenced by the temptation plot, the others being *Pacient Grissell*, a full scope comi-tragedy by Wager himself called *The Longer Thou Livest the More Fool Thou Art*, and four hybrid tragedies in which the plot reshapes literary sources: John Pickering's *Horestes*, Nathaniel Woodes's *The Conflict of Conscience*, and the other tyrant tragedies *Apius and Virginia* by "R. B." and *Cambises* by Thomas Preston. All of these exclude the traditional scene of the hero's realization of moral folly. We may readily understand how Pickering, Woodes, Phillip, Preston, and R. B. might have been disinclined to undertake the labor of imagining such a fundamental change in endings supplied by their literary sources—especially when for the tragic plays the endings were already perfectly in harmony with the Elizabethan didactic method of depicting as in a mirror the terrible reward of vice. Yet *Inough is as Good*, though not a hybrid but a direct adaptation of the second temptation of Mankynde in *The Castell of Perseverance*, likewise deviates from Mankynde's salutary recognition of the treachery of Coveytyse and this World. Worldly Man perishes deservedly, but unenlightened and therefore unredeemed in our eyes, his mind to the last "corrupt and il." The meaning of his death—the insidious and deadly spiritual peril of covetousness and ambition in magistrates—is patent to us but never to him. He dies in fact in the spiritual care of a chaplain whose name is Ignorance. Having watched a tempter with a disguise and false name deceive the Worldly Man by making greed look legitimate and moderation vicious, we are left unsatisfied when he falls still deluded. There is no psychological dénouement in Wager's play, for the knot of Worldly Man's folly remains tied. It is as if Mankynde were never to realize the falseness of Mundus and Coveytyse, or Macbeth that the sisters were equivocators and juggling fiends.

The sequence of events leading up to Worldly Man's death, brought about by a character called God's Plague distinctly related to Mankynde's nemesis Death, offers one of several links with the *Castell* drama which make Worldly Man's ignorance in death seem all the more exceptional and interesting. Wager in *Inough is as Good* and *The Longer thou Livest* is the last Tudor playwright to compose dramas of temptation partly on the original patterns without fusing them with story materials from nondramatic literature. But in doing so he hews more closely to the *Castell* play in certain respects than do, say, Skelton or even Medwall, to any known dramatic model. Worldly Man, whose name would fit Mankynde as he gathers treasure under the scaffold of the World, is betrayed into economic tyranny against the poor largely by his at first innocuous desire to be secure in old age. This is the path that led Mankynde into ruthless miserliness. The tempter is the same in both plays, Coveytyse, or "Covetouse" as the name is spelled in the Wager quarto, though he is now also called "the Vice." Mankynde too was unable to be content with "inowe," enough. There is talk in both plays about the merry time the executors will have; neither protagonist can leave his soul-purchased wealth to his wife and children. Nemesis strikes each just as he has proclaimed an act of climactic cruelty, and Wager indulges in the archaic touch of having Satan carry away Worldly Man's body much as Malus Angelus had carried Mankynde, or his soul Anima, toward Hell.

Worldly Man, smitten by the sword of God's Plague just as Mankynde was by the spear of Death, dies a similar lingering death, but his mind remains unpurged by any recognition of treachery. He believes to the end that his evil counselor is benevolent toward him. He is not privileged to learn the true name, and thereby the true nature, of his destroyer. Such benighted death is without precedent in plays of temptation composed before 1558, although it is characteristic from the beginning of Elizabethan tragedy.

To explain the disappearance of the recognition scene from the other tragic mutations of the temptation plot we may plead the

influence of literary sources or, more plausibly, the apparent inconsistency of regenerating the protagonist at the moment of his
deserved death. From *Wisdom* onward, the "recognycion" motivated
contrition and penance and thereby permitted the hero's restoration
to grace. But Wager has no literary source and follows most closely
the one theological drama of temptation (older than *Wisdom*) with
a recognition of moral truth that does not lead to contrition but only
to bitter awareness in death. The pattern of virtue, temptation, sin
survives more distinctly in *Inough is as Good* than in *Cambises*,
Pacient Grissell, and *Apius and Virginia*, largely because Wager
(despite the advertised "pleasant mirth") eschews the scenes of
vice-comedy that elsewhere break up the design and because Worldly
Man need not share the center of the play with an exemplary heroine.
Thinking that Covetouse is Policy and has only his welfare at heart,
Worldly Man is deeply deluded. Why does Wager substitute a
horribly dark death for the recognition called for by the tradition in
general and his model the *Castell* play in particular, as well as by the
audience's need to have its pent-up awareness of the deception
practiced upon Worldly Man given release through his realization
of it? Examination of the earlier phases of the plot suggests two
qualities of Wager's mind resisting the expected anagnorisis: his
own uncertainty about the moral truth of the protagonist's plight and
his Calvinistic sense of spiritual fatalism.

Wager invests with Tudor political and religious meaning what
had been a general allegory of Mankynde in his old age and of the
viciousness of worldliness. He gives the sin of the protagonist an
Elizabethan name, Ambition, and a topical coloring.[17] Presumably
Wager intends his protagonist to represent the class of early Elizabethan tyrannical magistrates, though Worldly Man is not explicitly
a former sufferer under Catholic oppression. "Wel chuse you, . . . doo
what you wil," says Inough immediately after, as if the hero, with
Mankynde's precious and perilous freedom, might follow the pattern
of these magistrates or not. Yet Inough's (and I think Wager's)
contradictory belief that the vice of worldliness or covetousness is
innate and ineradicable operates strongly in the play and at last
dominates. Wager is able to write one of the finest temptation scenes

in moral drama, in which Worldly Man is deluded by a brilliant Vice and turned from virtue to wickedness, from contentation to the restless ecstasy of covetousness, but not to write the other traditional pivotal scene that frees the protagonist's mind from the spell of evil. Worldly Man's nature and destiny become so to speak determined by his name, as those of Mankynde and Macbeth of course do not. The temptation plot, in other words, is here prevented from achieving a full rebirth in the realm of tragedy not by the influence of source but by that of Calvinism. What emerges is a tragic hero with good human instincts subtly intermingled with a strong penchant for covetous ambition who therefore can be blinded by the potent forces of evil abroad in his world. His spiritual enemies, introduced in the second scene according to the regular pattern of temptation plays, understand their man well ($B_{iv}v$) : though he now "studieth the rules of godly life erly & late," "verily he is inclined to be nought." Such a man might well play out the full design of Mankynde's old struggle with evil. But by the time of his death this inclination has gained such dominance that Worldly Man is a Mal Avisé, inaccessible to the moral truth.

The opening scene exposes Wager's concomitant uncertainty, echoed in the unenlightened catastrophe, as to what that truth may be with regard to wealth. Worldly Man is converted in this scene from a kind of neutral morality to a more positive, as if the Protestant playwright were unwilling to depict spontaneous or natural virtue not brought about by moral exhortation. Worldly Man enters "stout and frolike," a proud and happy man, but also thoughtful, not at all a tyrant, and discloses that he is "indewed with treasure" and seeks more. Men call him a worldly man, but he prefers their spite to their pity. He tells himself that he wants wealth for harmless purposes, so that he may have a merry old age, unlike that of his father who died poor and unregarded, and provide for his wife and children.

Now, judging from the Heywoodian proverb that is its title and from such names for virtues as Contentation and Inough, Wager means only to preach against excessive worldliness, not against worldliness per se. Actually he finds himself in the same dilemma that earlier had perplexed Skelton in *Magnyfycence*, the first Tudor play to teach the proper management of treasure. Wager and Skelton have in mind to praise moderation and show the folly and due punishment of excess. Magnyfycence spends too much and Worldly Man covets too much. But neither playwright is free from that medieval view which holds absolutely that all things of the world are vanity. Worldly Man "would be glad to doo for the best," but he is perplexed and inconsistent. He knows that Solon spoke cryptically to Cresus on the question of true happiness, seemingly saying that it consisteth after death. He declares that he will "take care which way and when" he gets treasure but can't resist adding that he *does* enjoy seeing a heap of old angels and crowns. When the zealous representatives of virtue chide him he yields and achieves what is presumably Wager's statement of the position of virtue with regard to riches:

> And indeed inough is as good as a feast,
> Good Lord how your woords have altred my minde:
> A new hart me thinks is entred in my brest,
> For no thought of mine olde in me I can finde.
>   I would to God you would take me in your company,
> And learne me how I may be an heavenly man:
> For now I perceive this world is but vanitie,
> Let a man therfore make of it as much as he can.
>   (B$_{ii}$r)

If it is proper to have "inough," and Contentation is a virtue, how can it be that the world is but vanity? Virtue now seems to be the extreme of otherworldliness: "I regarde neither treasure, Children nor wife" (B$_{ii}$r). Later in the play, however, during the phase of sin, Heavenly Man recalls this moment for the audience as follows:

> He promised you heard, from sin to arise,
> And said he would not loove neither money nor treasure,
> But as he ought to loove it, that is in a due measure.
>   (E$_{i}$r)

Wager's untenable position reminds us of Adversyte's criticism of

Magnyfycence: "Sometyme without Measure he trusted in gold." The opening scene of *Inough is as Good* conveys the impression that Worldly Man is a well-intentioned man unable to say in what, if anything, the right use of worldly wealth consists and that W. Wager is another.

This moral uncertainty returns in the catastrophe, helping there to block the expected recognition, but the middle phases of the play are relatively free from it because sin is represented by acts of outright tyranny, not by such practical, even humane worldliness as characterized Worldly Man at the outset. After the regular Introduction of Evil Agency, longer than usual because it is the chief vehicle for the pleasant mirth, Worldly Man enters to the Vice with his new companion Inough, like Macbeth with Banquo. Inough is able to intuit the true nature of Covetouse, while the flawed Worldly Man falls prey to his disguise, attractive pseudonym, and diabolic sophistry. With audacious irony, the Vice pretends to lament Worldly Man's new reputation for covetousness. With "inough" defined (through identification with miserliness) as an evil, fair is foul. Yet Worldly Man is less easily wrought upon than Gautier and most other heirs to Mankynde's role. The tempter must physically "pluck him back" from Inough. Precipitation (alias Redy Wit) suggests that a wealthy man may spread his benison widely, and "Policy" then introduces an insidious distinction among men which the Worldly Man is now inclined to accept:

> But yet Sir, riches to be good, wel proove I can.
> For every man is not called after one sorte:
> But some are called to prophecy, some to preach & exhorte.
> And he by that meanes Heaven joyes to win:
> But every man knoweth not that way to walke in.
> Therfore every man (as his vocation is) must walke.
>
> $(D_{iii}r)$

The Vice uses this specious distinction (echoed jokingly by Shakespeare's Falstaff) to hint that not all men are required to win Heaven, that wealth, now somehow his main theme, is a legitimate alternative. Worldly Man sees and confirms this implication: "The best heaven," he muses, ". . . is rich for to be" ($D_{iii}v$). He has for-gotten his own hazy understanding of the wisdom of Solon and become one of those men described in the first scene by Heavenly Man "that in riches account their blisse, / Beeing infected with Am-bition that sicknes uncurable" (B_iv). His words at once echo Mankynde's assertion that for riches' sake he is content "& nevere to comyn in heavyn" and anticipate Macbeth's willingness to jump the life to come.

From the start of the phase of Sin ($D_{iv}r$–$E_{iv}r$), Worldly Man betrays the same hypnotized passivity in the spell of Policy that characterizes Gautier under the influence of Politic Perswasion: "faith let him teache me what he wil: / And I wil doo it, if it were mine owne father to kil" (E_ir). The spell is never broken. Though we are given to understand that he is guilty of all the sins of a covetous man in authority, we see him as an oppressor of the poor, not, as might be expected, of God's ministers. Characters named Tenant, Servant, and Hireling express the hatred occasioned in them by the miser's injustices. Heavenly Man foretells God's wrathful reaction. The sinner has risen mercilessly in the scale of worldly prosperity until now, at the top of Fortune's wheel, proposing one more ruthless acquisition, he hears the voice of the "Prophet without."

At this point in any pre-Elizabethan interlude of temptation we should expect such a character as Verity or Knowledge of Sinne to admonish and enlighten the protagonist so that he might repent. Wager permitted Worldly Man a kind of recognition in the opening scene and caused him at the peak of virtue to allude to the text in Ezekiel that lends support to the scenes of moral awakening. God, Worldly Man said,

> wil not the death of Sinners as Scripture dooth say.
> It hath pleased him to open unto me the true light,
> Whereby I perceive the right path from the brode way.
>
> ($C_{iv}v$)

But now the Worldly Man is permitted no such light or perception, and his sickness and death are made more terrible by the ignorance in which he faces them. The Prophet, who is Jeremiah, instead of stating clearly the facts of Worldly Man's deception speaks his parable of the watchful and idle servants. Worldly Man is only troubled and perplexed: "Good Lord I wold know what these woords doo mene." To expound them he sends the figure whom he knows only as Policy to fetch the chaplain who he thinks is Devotion. While waiting he complains of his aching head and falls into a sleep troubled by the vision of God's Plague, represented for the audience by a sword-bearing figure who now enters and stands behind Worldly Man a while before speaking. Worldly Man hears that he will be filled with sickness, die, and be damned, that he sleeps "in death as the Prophet David doth say." The allusion to Psalms 13.3, ". . . lighten mine eyes, lest I sleep the sleep of death," shows the protagonist to be still in moral darkness. The information that "Straungers and those whome thou didst never knowe, / Shall possesse that, which by fraud thou hast got" clearly echoes the *Castell* playwright's use of the symbolic Boy named "I Wot Nevere Whoo," the recipient of all Mankynde's treasure. And as God's Plague describes himself and strikes Worldly Man with his sword, his kinship with Death in the older drama is plain:

> I go through all townes and Cittyes strongly walled,
> Striking to death and that without all mercy.
> Heer thou wicked covetouse person I doo strike—
>
> ($F_{ii}v$)

God sends his plague "Because at his Prophets preaching thou amendest not," no allowance being made for the parabolic nature of that preaching or Worldly Man's effort to have its meaning expounded for him. Wager perhaps intends to dramatize his Protestant conviction that Scripture is nowadays in neglect. But if Worldly Man has failed to achieve the insight and contrition that any earlier Tudor playwright would have granted him at this point, he might still achieve the bitter recognition, too late to return him to grace, that Mankynde had endured after the blow of Death. The most that Worldly Man ever comprehends is the certainty of his death. He still calls Covetouse Policy and Ignorance Devotion. These figures do not reveal their true natures and mock him, as they might now

safely do and as Mundus had done with such relish during the
corresponding part of the *Castell* play. His condition is exemplified
when in the midst of his sickness and terrible pains he declares to the
agent of his destruction: "I like not these foolish dreames, Policy
my freend." Waiting for Ignorance to bring a physician, he cries
out, "O Policy sick, never so sick . . . , / Oh sira, what shal become
of all my goods when I am dead?" and Covetouse turns to the
audience and interprets for them ($F_{iii}r$): "Lo, see you not how the
worldly man showeth his kinde? / As sick as he is, on his goods is
all his minde." The Physician, like the later Doctor of Physicke who
treats the similar case of Lady Macbeth, cannot minister to a mind
diseased. Worldly Man dies in a final gesture of worldliness, an
effort to dictate his will. God's name sticks in his throat and he falls
dead. Ignorance explains the matter to Covetouse:

> Tush, God: a strawe, his minde was other waies occupyed:
> All his study was who should have his goods when he dyed.
> Indeed all men may perceive his minde to be corrupt and il:
> For God would not suffer him to name him in his wil.
>
> ($G_i r$)

It is difficult to imagine what truths about the world and its
forces for evil Wager might have written for Worldly Man to say
had he not suppressed the recognition scene. The pat moralizing of
Inough, Contentation, and Heavenly Man that closes the play evades
the knotty issues in the protagonist's life. But the Worldly Man is
allowed no vision of truth. Covetousness becomes not so much a
tempter external to him as a part of his nature. By Calvinistic typing,
to the end he "showeth his kind." The Worldly Man will needs be
a Worldly Man still, and Ambition is a sickness incurable. There
could be no sharper contrast with the realization suffered by Mankynde and Macbeth which, though unavailing, clears their minds at
the last of all delusion and worldliness.

Cambises points toward Macbeth in his patriotic military prowess
and cruelty as a king, Apius in his inability to resist his own base
drives in an atmosphere of moral ambiguity, Worldly Man in his
insatiate ambition. None of them so fully establishes the pattern of

experience to be reenacted by Macbeth as had Mankynde himself in the *Castell* play. The efforts of a few playwrights at the very inception of English tragedy to create it in the image of the native temptation play were crude and short-lived. To vindicate what they had attempted, Shakespeare not only took the process past the hybrid stage but at the same time let the theological originals pervasively infuse and reshape the literary raw materials supplied him by Cinthio and Holinshed. That is why *Othello* is essentially closer to *Wisdom* than to *Pacient Grissell*, and *Macbeth* to the *Castell* play than to *Inough is as Good*.

CHAPTER III

Mankynde in Macbeth

If any man be fer or nye
    That to my servyse wyl buske hym boun,
If he wyl be trost and trye
    He schal be kyng and were the croun.
        —Proclamation of the World in
            The Castell of Perseverance

The Castell of Perseverance[1] stands at the head of the long tradition of English temptation plays of which the last is *Macbeth*. It stages in its round, universally symbolic theater the temptation of Mankynde from his initial innocence and virtue, his sin and tragic death, and at last transcends this tragic world to close in Heaven. The career of Macbeth is by far more deeply akin to the earthly part of the experience of his prototype Mankynde than to the experience of any intermediate protagonist, even though Mankynde's life be conceived in theological and allegorical terms. *Macbeth* stands in much the same relationship to the *Castell* drama that we shall find to align *Othello* with *Wisdom Who is Christ* and *King Lear* with *The Pride of Life.* Each of the great tragedies of human folly reembodies, out of materials derived from literary sources, a dramatic plot whose original terms were abstract and whose shaping conception was theological. Each, unlike the Tudor interludes, matches its prototype in its universality of scope and its religious meaning. The *Castell* play and *Macbeth* share a grandeur and moral seriousness lacking in any Tudor play except perhaps *Doctor Faustus;* we may say of them as did Goethe of Marlowe's play, "Wie gross ist alles angelegt."

Beyond this, Mankynde and Macbeth, first and last to play out the temptation plot, exhibit striking correspondences in stage careers separated by two centuries. The initial moral uncertainty of Macbeth, rooted in his flawed nature, the supernatural soliciting, the half-blind willingness to jump the life to come in return for a worldly throne, the ensuing career of falsehood and oppression all have their *Castell* prototypes. These and other, sometimes more particular resemblances place *Macbeth* nearer in conception to the *Castell* drama than to any Tudor play lying between them. Most centrally, Mankynde, like Macbeth, is led through metaphysical sophistry to believe that sin, though he well knows it to be sin, will somehow be best for him, all things considered. The moral play is much concerned with the error of this belief which together with Mankynde's bitter recognition of it as Nemesis overmasters him constitutes the major link with *Macbeth*.

Describing *Macbeth* as "a morality play written in terms of Jacobean tragedy," Farnham, thinking chiefly of the early Elizabethan moral plays turned tragic, rightly adds this qualification: "But *Macbeth* is unlike the normal morality for the reason that its hero begins his evil-doing with complete understanding of the course he is laying out for himself and with complete willingness to sacrifice his soul in the next world in exchange for the gifts of this world. He is deceived by supernatural agents of evil, but he is not blinded by them morally through the specious argument that vice is not truly vicious or that it is not repulsive, as the hero of the morality is usually blinded."[2] This is precisely the difference that distinguishes the *Castell* play from most of its successors in the tradition of the temptation play and at the same time joins it with *Macbeth*. Mankynde and Macbeth comprehend the moral significance of their course of action while deluded about the motives of their counselors. In the atmosphere of moral ambiguity evoked by the Weird Sisters, Macbeth supposes that what he knows to be foul may nevertheless be fair for him personally in its worldly consequences. He calls it "the Imperiall Theame" even as the thought of it, involving as it does "Murther," shakes his "single state of Man." He is divided like judge Apius, another rare exception to the general rule that the protagonist be deluded about the real sinfulness of his chosen behavior. Like Satan he falls by the sin of ambition, but we are able to sympathize with Macbeth because we see that he is fooled—even if the area of his delusion is not moral and if evil has done no more than prompt him to become self-deluded.[3]

The *Castell* playwright emphasizes the fact that Mankynde is

"gylyd . . . ful qweyntly" (l. 530), "bobbyd And blent" (l. 1287),
even though he knows all of his vicious companions by their true
names. He is blinded to their total hostility, patent to the audience,
toward himself. He is under a spell, induced in the first instance by
Malus Angelus, who pretends to be concerned about his welfare and
enjoyment of the world. Soon he is so thoroughly entranced that the
agents of evil scarcely need dissimulate in his presence their sole
motive of causing him to damn himself. Early in the action, as
Richard Southern remarks, the Sins "speak with cynical frankness
among themselves, and the whole effect is heightened because,
through it all, Mankind sits beaming from his throne, hearing every
word they say, yet missing the drift from the first to the last."[4] Thus,
as Southern points out, Coveytyse can say to the others ". . . Lete us
lullyn hym in oure lust / Tyl he be drevyn to dampnynge dust"
(ll. 1041–42), and yet Mankynde does not grasp that the Sin is his
enemy. In the deeper folly of his old age, when Mankynde has
waxed greedy and tyrannous, he still heeds Coveytyse because he
thinks that Coveytyse wants no more than to help him to insure
himself against the economic hazards of age. He is oblivious to the
equivocation which colors the words of the Sin:

> Com on, olde man, it is no reprefe
> That Coveytyse be the lefe.
> If thou deye at any myschefe
> It is thiselfe to wyth.
>   (ll. 2501–4)

It is out of his conviction that Coveytyse and all the worldly forces
are on his side that Mankynde espouses the sophistry that a course
of action may be sinful in the absolute but somehow good for him,
at least during this life. He is willing "nevere to comyn in hevene"
(l. 2777) but strives restlessly after "more and more" to make his
old age secure and to provide for his posterity. So does Macbeth,
and the tragic hero's bitter realization that he has been deluded by
"Jugling Fiends" matches Mankynde's ultimate perception of the
duplicity of this World and his agents. Not until the temptation
scene in the next moral play, *Wisdom*, is the central figure taught

the larger untruth that absolute evil is absolute good. This is the normal form of temptation henceforward. Its effect is to increase sympathy for the protagonist. As his delusion is less narrow and selfish, so the eventual reversal and recognition are at least potentially more moving, more pitiful and terrible. The artistic vindication of this normal pattern lies in the experience of Othello, not of Macbeth.

We shall have occasion to notice correspondences of the tragedy to the kindred allegorical play not simply in plot design but in related verbal echoes, images, and symbols. Thus Mundus proclaims that any man trusty and true in his service "schal be kyng" as the third Sister all hails Macbeth "that shalt be King hereafter." At the price of his soul he is indeed made king, robed accordingly in royal vestments ill-fitted to his humble humanity, and enthroned, high and miserable, on the scaffold of covetousness. In Shakespeare, this symbolic kingship becomes actual. The "rycchest robys" and "nobyl aray" to which the moral playwright so often calls attention because they are so inappropriate to Humanum Genus match Macbeth's royal robes. Kingship for each man equals sin, a denial of his proper nature and role in life. The robes also match the imagery of ill-fitting clothing discovered by Caroline Spurgeon[5] and revealed in its thematic relevance in a well-known essay by Cleanth Brooks, "The Naked Babe and the Cloak of Manliness."[6] The manliness too has its *Castell* equivalent, for Malus Angelus as part of his temptation urges Mankynde to be manly, by which he really means to be a transgressor of the proper limits to human action. The babe and more generally the image which Brooks discusses of the Child as symbol of the future have the most fascinating antecedent of all: the ever-present Garcio who accompanies the World. Not only must Mankynde acknowledge that the agents of evil sought only to gain his soul for the common enemy of Man, but, worse still, he learns that the acquisitions that cost him his soul cannot even be left to his heirs as he had hoped but must go to the strange Boy, thinly clothed and wearing a torn hood, who takes his treasure just as Shakespeare arranges that immediately "the Boy *Malcolme*" and eventually the nameless children of the line of Banquo shall inherit Macbeth's equally costly crown and sceptre—"with an unlineall Hand."

The "parcellys" or phases of Mankynde's experience may be set forth as follows:

Conspiracy of Mundus, Belyal, Caro	ll.	157–274
Mankynde innocent		275–326
Temptation by Malus Angelus (vs. Bonus Angelus)		327–455
Sin		456–1297
Recognition and regeneration		1298–1601
Mankynde virtuous (while evil reorganizes and lays vain siege to his "Castel of Goodnesse")		1602–2405
Conspiracy of Mundus and Avaricia (Coveytyse)		2406–2426
Temptation by Avaricia (vs. Largitas)		2427–2556
Sin		2557–2777
Recognition in death		2778–3128
Debate of the Daughters of God		3129–3649

The range of the action is analogous to that of the great mystery cycles, from naked innocence to judgment, and may well have been conceived on this analogy. The playwright does not always distinguish clearly between the biography of mankind the typical individual and the history of mankind the race, the subject of the cycles. Ontogeny recapitulates phylogeny.

The details of the action and its lesson (the distilled wisdom of a religious age: "Evyr at the begynnynge / Thynke on youre last endynge!") apply however to the human individual alone. It will be seen from the outline that the design of the *Castell* play consists essentially of two parallel temptation plays, one beginning from the hero's baptismal innocence, the other from his tested and mature virtue. In each, Mankynde is betrayed by what is false within (his Bad Angel and his Avarice), lapses into evils of which the root is covetousness, and awakens to his error when his heart is penetrated by the lance of the dark character Penitencia or Mors. The one recognition restores him to grace through the sacrament of penance. It is the other which is tragic.

Between the two sequential temptation plays, as Mankynde rests secure in the Castle, occurs the Prudentian battle of his Virtues against the Vices, and after them is appended the Debate or Parliament in Heaven. In neither of these does Mankynde himself directly participate, as a speaking character, though he remains in sight of the audience. These parts of the play are much more closely related to other medieval literature, dramatic and nondramatic, than are the two temptation plays. Since they are less original and do not dramatically involve Mankynde, who is the key feature of English moral drama, the Psychomachia and the Parliament perhaps should be regarded as vestiges of the very formation of that drama. At any rate, neither of them figures in the two later Macro plays or survives frequently or significantly in the long tradition of Tudor moral interludes of temptation.

Certain Tudor plays, from Medwall's *Nature* (1498) to W. Wager's *The Longer thou Livest* (ca. 1560), retain the doubleness of pattern as well as something of the fullness of scope of the *Castell* play. Traces of these features may be discerned in *Macbeth*. Macbeth meets twice with the Weird Sisters. He is first of all tempted to enter upon a course of evil and midway in the play "further tempted," as Farnham says, to confirm himself in this course and so destroy himself. He does not of course repent before his second plunge into evil-doing. Though to be sure Macbeth is not newly born at the beginning of his stage life, Shakespeare stresses his innocence through the comments of Lady Macbeth. In the terms of the imagery of seed and plant, Macbeth may indeed be said to begin life in Act I, for King Duncan remarks, "I have begun to plant thee, and will labour / To make thee full of growing" (I, iv, 28–29), and though he is not literally an old man at the end, his way of life "Is falne into the Seare, the yellow Leafe" (V, iii, 23) and he shall lack the comforts that "should accompany Old-Age."

Rather than preserving the features of the full scope play, the majority of Tudor moral interludes reduce it to a single design in which each phase of the hero's experience with temptation occurs only once and the whole occupies the crucial period in his maturity rather than spans his entire life. Such is the structure of W. Wager's other, and better, moral tragedy, *Inough is as Good as a Feast* (ca. 1560), which is indebted to the *Castell* play. This economical design predominates in *Macbeth*. The coalescence had occurred as early as *Wisdom* and *Mankind* in the fifteenth century. These Macro plays, and most other pre-Elizabethan temptation plays, resemble the first working out of the temptation pattern in the *Castell* play in that they end with the sacrament of penance, or some secular adaptation of it, and so restore their protagonists to grace. The Elizabethan moral tragedies more nearly resemble the second temptation play in *The Castell of Perseverance*, and on the whole Macbeth's career likewise parallels Mankynde's second fall into tyranny and sin. It is striking to find Mankynde, like Macbeth, flushed with his victory in a great military encounter, yet unable to resist a sophistical appeal to his self-interest and consequently deserting his proper castle to gain other "Howsys and homys, castell and cage" (l. 2495) and be a tyrant. Yet much in Mankynde's first encounter with deception and sin, notably his symbolic investment as a king, also finds its Shakespearean equivalent in *Macbeth*. Hence in comparing the great medieval and Renaissance dramas of sinful ambition we must set *Macbeth* against a background jointly composed of the two temptation plays which chiefly constitute *The Castell of Perseverance*.

The opening presents us with Mundus, Belyal, and Caro each seated upon his scaffold awaiting the entrance of Mankynde on the green or *platea*, which is the moral universe. The World boasts that all lands are his through his "tresorer, Syr Coveytyse" (l. 181). Belyal, "Satanas in my sad synne" he calls himself, cannot be content unless he lures Mankynde to Hell. Caro, "Mankyndys fayre Flesch" (l. 237), waits his chance to dispose him toward gluttony, lechery, and sloth. Thus the evil charm is wound up to the end that Mankynde make the worst use of his free will:

> Behold the Werld, the Devyl, and me!
> Wyth all oure mythis we kyngys thre,
> Nyth and day besy we be
>   For to distroy Mankende. . . .
>
> (ll. 266–69)

These are the malevolent trio that a man must deal with when he enters this life. Two of them do not speak again till much later in the play, and Southern thinks that they vanish behind their scaffold-curtains. But after Mankynde has been introduced and while he paces on the green below with his Good and Bad Angels, Mundus has two further stanzas of boasting. With him are two messengers and, judging from the *nomina ludorum*, Garcio, the "lythyr ladde with a torne hod" as the Prologue describes him (l. 109) who shall, like Banquo's issue, inherit all that the protagonist has risked damnation to get; Garcio, though he does not yet speak, is thus before the audience from the outset. It is here that the World speaks the figurative prophecy made literal by the Weird Sisters, that any man who trusts him "schal be kyng and were the croun / Wyth rycchest robys in res" (ll. 476–77).

The World, the Devil, and the Flesh thus introduced, though confessedly busy to destroy Mankynde, do not themselves propose to him any course of sinful behavior. They tempt him only in the sense of providing the environment in which he can so easily damn himself. As Mankynde enters beneath them he is truly innocent, what Belyal contemptuously calls "al holy Mankynne" (l. 218).[7] The playwright puts no Augustinian emphasis upon original sin and depravity. Though Mankynde was born "this nyth," he already wears upon his head (he wears nothing else) the "crysme . . . / that I tok at myn crystenynge" (ll. 294–95). He is "ful of thowth" concerning his miserable frailty and prays to Christ that of the two angels assigned to accompany him through life he may follow the Good Angel that came from Heaven's throne. Bonus Angelus hereupon encourages him to serve Jesu, "that deyed on rode for Mankynde," to his life's end, for then he shall not want. Mankynde's initial innocence and leaning toward good invite the moral suasion and deceit which are to become hallmarks of the temptation plays.

Moral struggle begins with the rejoinder of Malus Angelus, "Pes, aungel, thi wordys are not wyse!" (l. 340). Mankynde is rapt, "stylle as ston" (l. 345), listening to the contest for his allegiance between angels who represent his dual potential and spiritual links with Heaven and Hell. Bonus Angelus must make a case for self-denial. Malus Angelus counters that in God's service one cannot expect to have a fair lady, rich rents, and silk sandals. Mankynde

gives voice to the dilemma in which he finds himself plunged by
this angelic soliciting:

> Whom to folwe wetyn I ne may.
> I stonde and stodye and gynne to rave.
> I wolde be ryche in gret aray
> And fayn I wolde my sowle save
> As wynde in watyr I wave.
>
> (ll. 375–79)

But in truth he is hopelessly ensnared already by the appeal of his
worldly instincts, and the last argument of good, that he think about
his ending day when he shall be closed under clay, falls on deaf
ears. There will be time, he is led to believe, to worry about his
soul when he is sixty winters old. Now, "to the Werld us must gon,"
says Malus Angelus, and he adds at once: "And bere the manly
evere among" (ll. 435–36). Manliness, then, in the specious rhetoric
of evil is identified with worldliness. Mankynde will "be manly . . .
thou I be fals." Soon, before the scaffold of the World, he shall
declare his willingness to jump the life to come in exchange for
rewards in this life:

> Of my sowle I have non rewthe.
> What schulde I recknen of domysday
> So that I be ryche and of gret aray?
>
> (ll. 605–7)

And on that scaffold World's servants will invest him in the rich
robes of a king, emblematic of the state of sin.

The rising action of *Macbeth*, from the introduction of the Sisters
till Macbeth is "gone to Scone / To be invested" (II, iv, 31–32)
resembles the opening of the *Castell* play in its essentials and uniquely
in some of its details. In neither play do the external forces of evil
introduced in the first scene themselves subvert the protagonist. Instead they create the environment in which his private devil may
blind him and entice him to damn his eternal soul for a worldly
crown. Mundus tells his messengers to proclaim all through the land

that any man inclined to serve him "schal be kyng," but Mankynde is not actually welcomed into World's presence until he has already chosen to be rich and renowned here "be buskys and bankys broun" (l. 574) and forget about God. The personal struggle through which he arrives at that decision adumbrates Macbeth's soliloquies of soul-struggle and the scene with Lady Macbeth at the close of Act I in which she overcomes his scruples and fears with the specious argument from manliness employed by Malus Angelus. The Sisters, though they do speak to Macbeth upon his entrance and start or renew the thoughts that shake his single state of man, propose no course of evil action. It is simply given to 3. Witch to say, echoing the proclamation of Mundus, "All haile Macbeth, that shalt be King hereafter."

Early in each play our attention is directed to the instruments of darkness on two occasions, between which we catch our first glimpse of the protagonist, directly in the *Castell* play and indirectly through the praise of the bleeding Captain and of Ross in *Macbeth*. The three hags, bearded, withered, and wild in their attire as we know from Banquo's later description, bear no particular resemblance to Mundus, Belyal, and Caro. They are quite nonallegorical. But their entrance to the sound of thunder and lightning and the few words they exchange in "the fogge and filthie ayre" establish the atmosphere of moral ambiguity into which the protagonist must step and by which, his first words will presently imply, his mind is already permeated. They will meet with him in the twilight time when the battle (as in Mankynde's second temptation midway in the *Castell* play) is lost and won, lost morally though won militarily, typifying a world in which as Macbeth will see it "faire is foule, and foule is faire."

After the portrait of brave Macbeth supplied by Act I, scene ii, and just before he meets them, we learn something more of these malevolent powers. Evidently (judging from I, iii, 1–38) their occupation is to plague humanity. They are ubiquitous, "Posters of the Sea and Land," a quality of which Mundus especially boasts. But their powers are limited. The sailor's wife was able to say, "Aroynt thee, Witch," and though her sleepless husband shall "dwindle, peake, and pine" under 1. Witch's influence, "his Barke cannot be lost." Like the devils who torment the Old Man in *Doctor Faustus*, the Weird Sisters cannot destroy the soul. The implication, reinforced at once by the contrasting reactions of Macbeth and Banquo to the salutations of these imperfect speakers, is that a man must cooperate in his own perdition. A suggestion from within Macbeth's mind supplies the imperfection of their speech with the unspoken assumption that he must murder to be king and plunges him into moral struggle. Banquo, who recalls Wager's character Inough, instinctively associates them with "the Devill," a roughly accurate equation, and rightly guesses that they are "Instruments of Darknesse." Not until it is too late will Macbeth himself have the insight to realize that these whom he now regards as metaphysical aid to his designs are in fact "Jugling Fiends."

The sisters meet Macbeth, as he writes to his wife, "in the day of successe" in battle. As a victorious general who falls from grace through deceit because of his flawed nature, Macbeth resembles the mature and virtuous rather than the new-born Mankynde. But in some aspects of his character and in his reaction to evil suggestion he also bears comparison with Mankynde in his innocence. Lady Macbeth's description of his nature carries implications of innocence. "It is too full o' th'Milke of humane kindnesse, / To catch the neerest way" (I, v, 18–19). He is "not without Ambition, but without / The illnesse should attend it." This deficiency she is prepared to make up with the valor of her tongue. "What thou would'st highly," she apostrophizes, "That would'st thou holily," her term recalling as we have noted Belyal's scornful "Al holy Mankynne" (l. 218) and again "al holy Mankende" (l. 234). He seems a man as yet pure in deed, even holy, flawed only by the potentialities of an ambition that is the Renaissance equivalent of the general worldliness of Mankynde. The soul-struggle that engages him till the end of Act I bears out this description as well as resembles the conflict between Bonus and Malus Angelus.

The immediate outward effect of the prophecy upon Macbeth is to make him "start" and become "wrapt withall" (I, iii, 51, 57). This preoccupation is reasonably taken by critics to imply that Macbeth has thought ere this of being king, but also it aligns him with Mankynde, who says, "I stonde and stodye al ful of thowth," and who at the first words of Malus Angelus stands "stylle as ston." Shakespeare stresses it in Banquo's comment, "Looke how our Partner's rapt" (I, iii, 142), after Ross and Angus have hailed Macbeth Thane of Cawdor. And Macbeth writes to his wife that after the witches vanished into air he "stood rapt in the wonder of it." At first we can only guess the process of his thought, but in the long aside (I, iii, 130–42) we learn that it consists of a "suggestion" that divides his single state of man and of reaction that involves a failing effort to distinguish "good" from "ill." Macbeth to be sure has no visible Malus Angelus to make the suggestion, although for one scene (I, vii) his dearest partner in villainy may be said to take the role and although just before his death Macduff makes reference to "the Angell whom thou still hast serv'd." In effect, Macbeth indeed has served his Bad Angel as does Mankynde, from the moment he yields to the suggestion of sin until the stroke of death. Macbeth's asides and the soliloquy of Act I, scene vii, however, are an alternative convention to the old debate of the two angels, preserved half-heartedly by Marlowe in *Doctor Faustus*, for dramatizing inner struggle. The technique for representing such struggle in *Apius and Virginia* is perfectly transitional: Conscience and Justice are actually present and visible on stage but silent, while the protagonist soliloquizes.

In the first aside, while Banquo chats with Ross and Angus, we discover that Macbeth's mind is already half-deluded and half-possessed by worldly aspiration, by what he calls "the Imperiall Theame." His "single state of Man" is so shaken by his inner struggle "That Function is smother'd in surmise." The struggle is between his good instincts and his bad. His innate goodness makes the image suggested to him by his thoughts "horrid," his imaginings "horrible." The horrid image unfixes his hair and makes his seated heart knock at his ribs. But his own worse nature made the suggestion to which he yields. He, not the Weird Sisters, introduces the term "Murther" into the play, and though he speaks of "supernatural solliciting" it is really his own mind that solicits him. This soliciting, he muses,

> Cannot be ill; cannot be good.
> If ill? why hath it given me earnest of successe
> Commencing in a Truth?   (I, iii, 131–33)

Evidently he has paid no heed to Banquo's cry a few lines earlier,
"What, can the Devill speake true?" nor to Banquo's equally sound
intuition that the Sisters are "Instruments of Darknesse," nor the
sound advice that oftentimes such instruments

> tell us Truths,
> Winne us with honest Trifles to betray's
> In deepest consequence.   (I, iii, 124–26)

Macbeth yields to a sophistry of his own making when he surmises
that "ill" must be inconsistent with "earnest of successe, / Com-
mencing in a Truth."

The soliloquy of moral struggle (I, vii, 1–28), spoken while
Duncan sups his last, discloses Macbeth's willingness to reck not of
Doomsday (to "jumpe the life to come") in exchange for rewards
in this world ("heere, upon this Banke and Schoole of time"). This
is equivalent to Mankynde's willingness to neglect his soul so that
he "be ryche and of gret aray." Later, his awareness that he has given
his soul to the common enemy of man contributes to Macbeth's
misery as the rewards of sin prove increasingly hollow even in the
here and now, as they do for Mankynde. But though Mankynde
(through his Good Angel) and Macbeth think primarily of the
consequences to themselves of sin or crime, it is the prospect of
"judgement heere" rather than in the afterlife that actively deters
Macbeth.

> This even-handed Justice
> Commends th'Ingredience of our poyson'd Challice
> To our owne lips.   (I, vii, 10–12)

Conscience too speaks in secular rather than in religious terms. Mankynde's Good Angel urged him to "serve Jhesu, hevene kynge" who
lent him life and died on the cross. Macbeth's better nature reminds

him of his obligations as kinsman, subject, and host to Duncan, who

> Hath borne his Faculties so meeke; hath bin
> So cleere in his great Office, that his Vertues
> Will pleade like Angels, Trumpet-tongu'd against
> The deepe damnation of his taking off.
>
> (I, vii, 17–20)

Each soul-struggle ends in a specious appeal by the voice of temptation to manliness and in the protagonist's assertion that he will play
false. Malus Angelus says "thou muste be fals / Amonge kythe and
kynne" (words equivalent to Lady Macbeth's "looke like th'innocent
flower, / But be the Serpent under't") and "bere the manly evere
among," Mankynde replying as we have seen with a promise to "be
manly" and "fals." Macbeth, if it were only a question of vaulting
ambition against duty and fear of consequences, would proceed no
further in the business. But Lady Macbeth enters, and though in her
love for him she is no Malus Angelus seeking his damnation, the
argument she uses to win him to crime is the old argument from
manliness. "Art thou affear'd," she asks,

> To be the same in thine owne Act, and Valour,
> As thou art in desire? Would'st thou have that
> Which thou esteem'st the Ornament of Life,
> And live a Coward in thine owne Esteeme?"
>
> (I, vii, 39–42)

When he counters that to dare more than may become a man is to
be none, she replies that when, presumably before the play, he broke
the enterprise to her he was a man, "And to be more then what you
were, you would / Be so much more the man." He has sworn, she
alleges, and if he screws his courage to the sticking place they'll not
fail. After the soul-struggle Macbeth is settled, and he whose face
was once open as a book departs with his wife on the line, "False
Face must hide what the false Heart doth know." So Mankynde,
departing with Malus Angelus, declared "and thou I be fals, I ne

recke" (l. 440)—providing he be enabled to live like a lord. Soon the air-drawn dagger marshals Macbeth the way that he has decided to go, and by killing the king he gains kingship which, for him as for Mankynde, is a state of sin.

Macbeth, to be sure, does not fall so much from baptismal innocence as from the established virtue of middle age, and in this respect his lapse from grace matches Mankynde's second lapse, occurring after Shrift has assoiled him and sent him to the Castle. As in *Macbeth*, evil suggestion wins the day after a glorious martial victory for the powers of good.

The pattern by which evil loses in battle and wins through guile comes to the *Castell* playwright from the *Psychomachia* of Prudentius, who had in mind not only the battles of classical epic which he allegorized but the careers of Judas and, more pertinently, of Achar who, as Prudentius says, "fell in the midst of victory. For though he won glory by the slaughter and was exalted by the overthrowing of the walls, he fell a victim to the gold that was taken from the beaten foe."[8] Prudentius has no character like Mankynde, who is evidently an invention of the moral playwrights. The field of battle is itself the human soul. After an invocation to Christ, the Vices and Virtues fight in pairs, Fides versus Idololatria, Pudicitia versus Libido, and so forth, each Virtue emerging victorious. Then Avaritia, like Coveytyse in the play, decides to try deceit. Why not use trickery, she reasons, having failed in the clash of battle? "Nil refert armis contingat palma dolisve" (l. 550). She changes her appearance to that of the Virtue men call Frugality or Thrift and bewilders the Virtues—much as Macbeth is bewildered—by her equivocal aspect (*biformis portenti*) of enemy and friend. But Operatio kills her, and so the *Psychomachia* does not finally resemble a temptation play.

By an interesting coincidence, the moral playwright divides the assault into two phases, so that Mankynde's victory, like Macbeth's as described in Act I, scene ii, is two-fold. The first assault is led by Belyal; the second wave is of the sins of Caro, the flesh. The rowdy mustering of the forces of evil, their comic and horrible uncouthness, the hurly-burly of alarums and excursions, and the noise of trumpets, firecrackers, and bagpipes together with the charm of the speeches of the lady Virtues make this psychomachia one of the most memorable passages in medieval drama.[9]

As the din of warfare subsides, Mankynde like Macbeth quietly loses to the sophistry of his own mind all that he has won through the militance of his virtues. His Evil Angel, always in charge of the strategy of evil, turns to Mundus, the world, who assigns Covetyse to work in his best wise and lure Mankynde out of the Castle and away from "yone vertuse all."

> Now [as Southern recreates the scene] comes what must have been one of the most dramatic moments of the play. With the triumphant Ladies, flushed with victory, aloft around Mankind on the tower; with the six Sins spread in a circle of misery round the Castle-foot, licking their wounds; with Flesh and the Devil fuming, sullen and despondent; . . . —Covetyse walks slowly out on his own and calls Mankind very softly and reasonably.[10]

Why not come out of that cold Castle (so his argument runs) and be among men? During the long psychomachia, we discover, Mankynde has begun to grow old. And the issue that now confuses him until he is willing once again to risk damnation is not manliness but security. Though Coveytyse does not hide behind the name or the appearance of Thrift, his promise is a deception of similar force: "The ryth wey I schal the teche / . . . to thryfte" (ll. 2477–78). Mankynde wonders what is the right way, for he does not know what to do now in the decrepitude of old age. That is just the time to lay aside a little something, Coveytyse argues, some marks and pounds, lands, houses, and so forth. And he adds with subtle irony in lines already noted that should Mankynde die when about any mischief, he shall have only himself to blame. It is good, Mankynde muses (ll. 2541–43)—that is, good for him within the bounds of this life, not morally good or good for his soul:

> It is good, whouso the wynde blowe,
> A man to have sumwhat of his owe,
> What happe so-evere betyde.

As the Good Angel cries out helplessly to the sweet Ladies, Man-kynde forsakes them.

The sequence of virtue proven in martial victory then lost to the sophistry of evil recurs, quite divorced from allegory, in *Macbeth*. Having set before us the three instruments of darkness, the dramatist immediately takes pain to create an image of Macbeth the mag-nificent warrior, whose worth on the field of battle in his country's behalf is manifest in the breathless accounts of the Sergeant and of Ross and whose loyalty stands in contrast with the treachery of the formidable Macdonwald and of Cawdor. It is "brave *Macbeth* (well hee deserves that Name)," "(Like Valours Minion)," "valiant Cousin, worthy Gentleman," "Bellona's Bridegroome, lapt in proofe," "Noble *Macbeth*." An actual presentation of the battles would be inefficient and, so near the start of the play, incomprehensible. But the wounded Sergeant, fresh from the field where the issue was still in doubt, lends his own immediacy to his account of it, com-pleted a moment later by Ross. The scene does more than initiate the theme and imagery of blood and inform us before the witches hail Macbeth that Glamis is now Cawdor. It defines the particular height of merit from which Macbeth is to be tempted. A sense of the protagonist at his finest is required if his temptation is to have significance and his transgression to offer tragic contrast. Act I, scene ii, together with the praises lavished on Macbeth later in the act, the portrait by his wife, and the glimpses of virtues of character that we catch in his soliloquies, supplies this sense. His nature com-bines heroic bravery and the milk of human kindness but is flawed to the very center by ambition, without as yet the "illnesse," evilness, that should attend it if he is to turn from virtue to vice.

Like Mankynde, Macbeth, though still perhaps "lapt in proofe," in the next scene begins to lose to the glosings of evil all the honor he has won in battle. Rapt and silent in the spell created by the three bearded women, he begins within his mind the dialogue through which eventually he will persuade himself to violate his own better nature and all his responsibilities as kinsman, subject, and host. The "suggestion," the "Thought," that shakes his "single State of Man" more nearly resembles that proposed by Malus Angelus than that of

Coveytyse, and it also leads to something closer to Mankynde's earlier
period of sin than to his later, because of the metaphor of kingship
and royal robes that the medieval playwright has now dropped. Yet
Macbeth's descent from virtue bears some generic resemblances to
Mankynde's fall into covetousness beyond the fact that it comes on
the eve of victory. There are of course no lady Virtues and Good
Angel to resist and lament Macbeth's decision in favor of treason.
(It is Duncan's "Vertues," Macbeth imagines, who "Will pleade
like Angels, Trumpet tongu'd" against the act of murdering him.)
But the pleasure that Mankynde takes in their company has its
parallel in Macbeth's pleasure in being admired:

> I have bought
> Golden Opinions from all sorts of people,
> Which would be worne now in their newest glosse,
> Not cast aside so soone.   (I, vii, 32–35)

Mankynde's last objection to Coveytyse is similar:

> I wyl not do these ladys dyspyt
> To forsakyn hem for so lyt.
> To dwellyn here is my delyt;
> Here arn my best frendys.
> (ll. 2514–17)

Macbeth, although old age is not yet an issue in his mind as it is
in Mankynde's, later perceives that because of his tyranny he must
not look to have the proper attributes of "Old-Age" including
"troopes of Friends." And a damning illusion of worldly security,
though not financial, is central to Macbeth's spiritual dilemma as to
Mankynde's. The guarantees that the Sisters seemingly provide lure
him onto and steady him upon his path of self-damnation. Hecate
(III, v, 32–33) generalizes in words applicable to the situation of
either protagonist: "Security / Is Mortals cheefest Enemie." Mankynde will become a ruthless land-grabber. A preoccupation with
tyranny as a source of security that is no security at all is of the
essence of Macbeth's condition after the murder of Duncan.

Whereas Macbeth goes to Scone to be invested, Mankynde goes to the scaffold of Mundus. There he gives his pledge to forsake God's service so that he may "regne rychely," and the World's servants Folly and Lust-Liking dress him in royal robes that cover the fleshings representative of new-born innocence. Backbiter (Detraccio) leads him thence to his throne on the northeast scaffold of Coveytyse, where he is welcomed with unctuous hospitality: "Sit up ryth here in this se . . ." (l. 834). Coveytyse details the cruelty and falsehood appropriate to a worldly man, which Mankynde willingly embraces, then calls for the Deadly Sins to gather, Pride, Wrath, and Envy from the northern platform of Belyal; Lechery, Slawth, and Glotony from the southern scaffold of the Flesh. These six colorful figures promenade to the foot of Mankynde's throne, one by one present themselves to him, gain acceptance, and climb the ladder of the scaffold to join his court. He shall reign with them until Penance reaches up from the green with a long lance and touches his heart.

Act II of *Macbeth*, given to the murder of Duncan, its discovery and immediate consequences, as we should expect, bears little detailed resemblance to the corresponding part of the *Castell* drama. The Bad Angel's escorting of Mankynde to the World, his investment, and his assignment to Backbiter to teach him the way to his throne, that is, are only broadly equivalent to the events between Macbeth's surrender to the immoral suasion of his wife and his entrance *"as King"* near the start of Act III. Yet the moral dramatist's choice of Backbiter as guide to the throne, a choice which must be intended to have general allegorical significance, calls attention to the fact that sovereignty falls on Macbeth (II, iv) because Malcolm and Donalbain are slandered with the imputation of unnatural and thriftless ambition. Macbeth himself in the next scene calls them "our bloody Cozens." This detraction anticipates that which (in IV, iii) Malcolm first speaks and then unspeaks of himself. Backbiter among men, be it noted, speaks "fayre beforn and fowle behynde" (l. 664), and Macbeth upon his first appearance in royal array speaks fair of Banquo to his face, calling his counsel always "both grave, and prosperous," and later in the same scene slanders him behind his back, as it were, to the two murderers.

In his second period of sin, Mankynde walks hand in hand with Coveytyse on the green rather than sits on the scaffold of that sin. This period is shorter than the first and its quality expressed more through choric comment than action and pageantry. The Virtues whom Mankynde has abandoned in the Castle exonerate themselves. Mankynde, they assert, is responsible, "Hymselfe may hys sowle spylle." "God hath yovyn him a fre wylle" (ll. 2558, 2560). The world's weal, he will discover, like a three-footed stool "faylyt a man at hys most nede," and Mundus himself, looking down from his scaffold echoes them (ll. 2698–99): "In hys most nede I schal hym fayle, / And al for Coveytyse." The Virtues can only wonder why Mankynde cannot appreciate the fact that body and soul shall inevitably part asunder. All this while, presumably, the Boy with the torn hood stands next to Mundus waiting to inherit what Mankynde has given his soul to receive. Malus and Bonus Angelus, respectively, gloat and lament.

On the plain Coveytyse tells Mankynde always to sing "more and more" and gives him a thousand marks, which he is not to share with the needy before he is graved under the green grass. He buries it where it will lie safe and sound, as he says, though his neighbor should hang for need of some of it. But a worldly man is never content:

> Yyt am I not wel at ese.
> Now wolde I have castel wallys,
> Strong stedys and styf in stallys,
> Wyth hey holtys and hey hallys. . . .
>
> (ll. 2747–50)

Coveytyse outdoes himself in a last speech, to this effect: "Lo, you've extorted cliff and coast, tower and town from your neighbors. Keep wanting more and more until you're dead and drop down. All this world won't quench your covetousness." The deluded protagonist fails to see through even this transparent speech, and his last words before Death (in place of Penance now) wounds him restate his blind willingness to jump the life to come:

> If I myth alwey dwellyn in prosperyte,
> Lord God, thane wel were me.
> I wolde, the medys, forsake the
> And nevere to comyn in hevene.
>
> (ll. 2774–77)

Despite the narrowing to avarice alone, the characteristic vice of old men, the quality of Mankynde's spirit is not essentially different in the two phases devoted to his sin. In each he is primarily with Coveytyse, in each he is blinded to the real motives of his advisors though knowing them by their true names. Each is distinctly a condition of prosperous misery. In youthful sin Mankynde is tyrannous and unjust (see ll. 746–50 for example), and Malus Angelus can remark of him (ll. 811–12), "Tyl man be dyth in dethys dow / He seyth nevere he hath inow," just as if it were the aged Mankynde. The dramatist heavily foreshadows the coming of Death to Mankynde even during this first phase of his sin. Thus Malus Angelus in delivering him to the World boasts openly, "I have gylyd hym ful qweyntly, . . . And whanne he wenyth best to lywe / Thanne schal he deye and not be schrywe / And goo wyth us to hell" (ll. 530–47). The playwright, had he so wished, by omitting the scene in which Mankynde is shriven might have proceeded directly through sin to death. For purposes of comparison with *Macbeth*, Mankynde's second period in sin may be regarded as continuous with his first.

Apart from the fundamental resemblance that for both Mankynde and Macbeth kingship, figurative or literal, is sin, the memorable details associating themselves with Duncan's murder—the air-drawn dagger, the blood, the fear of sleeplessness, the disruption of nature, even Duncan's horses "Contending 'gainst Obedience, as they would / Make Warre with Mankinde," bear no special relationship to Mankynde's inaugural sins or to their consequences. But as soon as Macbeth is king he exhibits something very like the misery of Mankynde growing out of restless dissatisfaction with his condition. Even when Mankynde is young in sin and has no deep sense of

insecurity, still, as we have seen, "he seyth nevere he hath inow."
He must, as Coveytyse himself says (l. 861), always gather "and
have non reste." Similarly Lady Macbeth finds (III, ii, 5) that
nothing is gained "Where our desire is got without content," and
her husband seconds her in bemoaning his mind's "restlesse extasie."
Seemingly, at least with Macbeth himself, this restlessness or dis-
content has a more specific cause than Mankynde's: Banquo, "Whose
being I doe feare." But the soliloquy (III, i, 48–71) in which he
says so, our first glimpse into his sorry state of mind as king of
Scotland, though it begins "To be thus, is nothing, but to be safely
thus," is finally concerned neither with fear nor safety. Banquo is
not a threat to his safety. The cause to which Macbeth finally lays
his disease of mind is that Banquo's children shall be kings. "For
Banquo's Issue have I fil'd my Minde," he thinks, and for this he has
given his soul "to the common Enemie of Man, / To make them
Kings. . . ." But it was clearly not for them, but to make himself
king, that Macbeth defiled his mind and gave his soul to Satan. It
is destiny that Fleance shall escape and his descendants, the seed of
Banquo, rule in Scotland. But this aspect of the hereafter has no
bearing on Macbeth's being "safely thus," as his muddled thoughts
evidently suppose, and his suborning of murderers to kill Banquo and
Fleance is nearly as irrational as his later attack on the wife and babes
of Macduff. Truly he has as he says put rancors in the vessel of his
peace, but his efforts to purify it are irrelevant and only charge his
soul the more with blood. His restless ecstasy is part of his being king,
like Mankynde's condition as he describes it from his throne in a
choric speech:

> Mankynde I am callyed by kynde,
>   Wyth curssydnesse in costys knet,
> In sowre swettenesse my syth I sende,
>   Wyth sevene synnys sadde beset.
>   (ll. 1238–41)

Below, on the plain, the Good Angel laments that Mankynde per-
versely slays his own soul, ruled (l. 1262) "aftyr the fende that is
thi foo," the common enemy of Man.

The restless dissatisfaction of a life in sin, the sour sweetness or doubtful joy as Lady Macbeth calls it, is more intensely felt and more closely, though still speciously, linked to motives of fear and safety when Mankynde is old. Despite his greater than Shakespearean emphasis on the pains of Hell in the life to come, the medieval dramatist clearly sees a career of worldly acquisitiveness as constituted of endless anxiety in the here and now. Coveytyse tempted Mankynde from the Castle of Virtue by evoking the insecurity of old age, but the motive of securing comfort immediately dissolves into an insatiate quest for "more and more" without rational basis. It involves, again irrationally, cruelty to others. Though a man should starve in a cave or hang on high, Avaricia urges, Mankynde must not help him, and finally it is as if he had acquired all the visible world—"Al this good, take the to, / Clyffe and cost, toure and toun"—and done so "Of thyne neygborys, be extorcyoun" (ll. 2754–57). Mankynde says that he can never say enough, enough. Immediately (l. 2724) he begs Coveytyse, "Yeve me good inow, or that I dey," but having received a thousand marks in gold and buried it he finds himself still "not wel at ese." His last speech before Death strikes him begins: "Qwenche nevere no man may; / Me thynkyth nevere I have inow. . . ." Shakespeare describes precisely the condition of Mankynde when he has Malcolm impute to himself

> A stanchlesse Avarice, that were I King,
> I should cut off the Nobles for their Lands,
> Desire his Jewels, and this others House,
> And my more-having, would be as a Sawce
> To make me hunger more, that I should forge
> Quarrels unjust against the Good and Loyall,
> Destroying them for wealth.   (IV, iii, 78–84)

Macduff's reply that such avarice "hath bin / The Sword of our slaine Kings," the thing which killed them, links it to Macbeth's ambition. Macbeth actually betrays the restless illogic of paranoia rather than of avarice. But he too is never at ease. His misdirected quest for peace in violence leads only deeper into sin as does Mankynde's unquenchable, destructive, and finally meaningless worldliness. These protagonists share much the same anxiety and the deadly philosophy that somehow, as Macbeth phrases it (III, ii, 55), "Things bad begun, make strong themselves by ill."

Macbeth's career of transgression is divided by the scene of his second encounter with the witches into two parts. This division is very likely a survival of the two-part structure of the full scope moral dramas from the *Castell* play onward. All of them, through Medwall's *Nature* to Wager's *The Longer Thou Livest*, preserve the tandem design of the *Castell* play, which is indeed a more clearly marked feature of these plays than is fullness of scope. In Wager's early-Elizabethan full scope drama, the hero, Moros, is no longer regenerated by realization and contrition as were Mankynde and Medwall's protagonist Man, so that his sins of old age involve rededication to folly rather than a return to it from a plateau of virtue. This modification is repeated in *Macbeth*, constituting a major deviation from the pattern of Mankynde's experience. Macbeth enjoys no period in middle life corresponding to Mankynde's stay in the Castle of Perseverance, no period with what Malcolm (IV, iii, 91) calls "The King-becoming Graces," among whom are "Patience" and "Lowlinesse," lady Virtues of Mankynde, as well as "Justice, Verity, Temp'rance, Stablenesse, / Bounty" and, most relevantly, "Perseverance." But otherwise Macbeth's life in sin significantly resembles the two-part configuration of Mankynde's. I have already indicated possible vestiges of the full scope range in his career, as in the botanical metaphor that takes him from the newly planted to a way of life fallen into the sere, the yellow leaf. Though he is not born into the play "in blody ble" like Mankynde, his experience as we know of it begins bloodily. It is also in connection with his first crimes, the murders of Duncan and Banquo, that we find as in Mankynde's entry into sin the false equation between being a man and doing evil. In their second phase his crimes wax more generally tyrannical, without any trace of the milk of human kindness in his nature as at first. Tyranny he undertakes as does aged Mankynde in the interest of security, "Mortals cheefest Enemie," and though it causes Macbeth to "scorne Death" as Hecate intended, it leads not only to isolation from humankind but to a dreary death that is the just consequence of his chosen way of life. In the banquet scene (III, iv), his last appearance until the bloody Child and the crowned Child lure him on to self-destruction, Macbeth boasts, "I am a man againe," and he closes the scene with the remark: "We are yet but yong indeed" (presumably "in deed"). It is in his next appearance after seeing the Sisters that Macbeth compares his position in life to the yellow leaf and laments the loss of "that which should accompany Old-Age."

Both of Mankynde's excursions into sin terminate in realization of the human folly that it involves; both recognitions are initiated when a dark figure on the *platea* reaches Mankynde's heart with his lance or spear. Unlike the lives in sin themselves, however, the awakenings to moral truth are otherwise fundamentally different in their natures and consequences, as Penitencia and Mors are different. Instead of combining qualities of each, *Macbeth* deviates altogether from the ending of the first of the temptation plays in the *Castell* sequence and ends in something very like Mankynde's bitter experience with Death.

Mankynde's growing and futile realization in his dying moments that he has been duped by the powers of spiritual darkness may indeed be called the allegorical type in English drama of Macbeth's tragic recognition. Unlike the endings of the later Macro plays *Wisdom* and *Mankind*, it lacks penitence and the cleansing tears that enable a return to grace. It disengages him from faith in this world, but without providing relief from the barren consequences of his having lived in such faith. True, he had always been willing, or thought he was, to forsake God's meeds for worldly prosperity. He was under no illusions about the probable fate of his soul. But he was under the illusion that worldliness would offer comfort until his soul must be damned and, we now discover, that his prosperity would pass into the lineal hands of children of his own blood. Bringing before him too late, and unavailingly, the total futility of his career as a worldly man, Mankynde's recognition is salutary only in a tragic sense. Unlike the corresponding experience earlier in his life, and in *Wisdom*, *Mankind*, and all the Tudor moral interludes before 1558, as well as in *Everyman*, it is not salvific. The salvation of Mankynde's soul, with which the play finally closes, is in other words altogether gratuitous. The speeches which extend the action beyond death ultimately cancel our sense of wasted spiritual potential, it is true. But the theatrical experience of the audience that witnessed Mankynde's bitter awakening in the presence of Death, the World, and the cruel Boy named "I-know-not-who" must have been one of total loss of noble potential. Even when the Soul comes out from under Mankynde's bed at the body's death and dares to hope in a last speech that somehow Mercy will overcome Justice, the impression is one of spiritual loss, especially as the Malus Angelus speaks his five horrifying stanzas on the pangs of Hell. Only insofar as the audience might recall the plot summary in the Proclamation read in the town a week earlier had they reason to suppose that the tragedy, having happened, might be annulled. Long after Mankynde's and the Soul's last words have been spoken and the action has been lifted to a realm beyond that of man and beyond that of the forces of evil, only then, in a close decision, do the ladies Mercy and Peace persuade their Father to let them take the Soul from the edge of Hell and lead it to the eastern scaffold where it may sit at his right hand.

No later English play about the temptation of its protagonist pursues the spiritual issue to its ultimate resolution in the life to come. None in fact, not even *Nature*, the next of the so-called full scope dramas, touches death, until certain early Elizabethan tragic interludes of temptation restore it. Always, until about 1558, the heir to Mankynde's role undergoes some kind of spiritual regeneration and regains grace more or less in the prime of life, as Mankynde had done at the close of his first venture into sin. Hence it is mis-leading to classify the *Castell* play with the succeeding dramas of temptation written before Elizabethan times as a group that end according to mercy, not according to mundane justice, for their errant protagonists. One must make a distinction between what Macbeth calls "both the Worlds," between justice here and in the life to come. Mors kills Mankynde not in the course of nature, though Mankynde is old, but because he has led a bad life and deserves to be struck down. There is nothing like this in later moral drama until the period when W. Wager's protagonists are killed by God's

Plague and God's Justice, dramatic descendants of Mors. Worldly Man and Moros, however, like Cambises, Apius, Philologus, and for that matter Faustus, perish with minds unpurged by the extensive recognition that Mankynde (and Macbeth) suffers. Mankynde and Macbeth alone die enlightened and yet unredeemed.

Mors, entering the arena, wins the attention of the audience from Mankynde. The five stanzas of Death's speech constitute one of the circulating speeches of the play, as Southern calls them,[11] one stanza to be spoken at his entrance through the gap, one for each of the four quarters of the circle as he makes his progress counterclockwise around it, arriving finally at the platform of the World where Mankynde stands enthralled by Coveytyse. Thus an awareness of Death's presence permeates to all the audience before Mankynde himself feels it in his heart. Often the medieval playwright achieves by such a shift of attention from one set of characters to another performing simultaneously in his spacious theater an effect that Shakespeare must build up by sequential scenes. Death's sixty-five lines spoken as Mankynde continues oblivious in sin create an impression of gathering nemesis. It corresponds to our sense first aroused at the close of Act III and intense by the close of Act IV that Macbeth "Is ripe for shaking, and the Powres above / Put on their Instruments." As with Mankynde, the resulting catastrophe will involve increasingly bitter recognition, without tears or any efficacy to save him, of the futility of his way of life and of the duplicity of those metaphysical beings who tricked him into choosing it and seemed to give it sanction.

Death, "drery Dethe" he calls himself, finds it high time to strike down Mankynde because "Mekyl of hys lyf he hath myspent" and because "He hathe hole hys hert on Coveytyse." He represents, then, "judgement heere" "upon this Banke and Schoole of time." Mors has for "Lordys and ladys in every londe" a "lessun" to teach (ll. 2794–95), and he says of Mankynde standing confidently with Coveytyse (l. 2832): "A newe lessun I wyl hym teche." If we take literally his cry that he raps Mankynde "To thyne herte rote," and especially if "drery" retains its Old English force of "bloody," the reaction to Mankynde's sins as to those of Macbeth is one of "Bloody Instructions."

The voice of Death and the sudden pain in his heart move the aged Mankynde to poetry: "A, Deth, Deth! drye is thi dryfte. / Ded is my destenye" (ll. 2843–44). But still he does not really understand what is happening, for he still trusts the World. His degree of understanding is analogous to that of Macbeth when we meet him in Act V. We last saw Macbeth in the witches' cavern, and despite his imprecation there, "Infected be the Ayre whereon they ride, / And damn'd all those that trust them" (IV, i, 138–39), now he does continue to trust "The Spirits that know / All mortall Consequences" (V, iii, 4–5), even as he hears from the whey-faced servant of the approach of the English. At the same time, however, as he tells Seyton, he is sick at heart. Speaking as if suddenly he had grown old like the hero of a full scope play, he shows that he at least realizes that living as a tyrant has not given him what he wanted of life:

> I have liv'd long enough: my way of life
> Is falne into the Seare, the yellow Leafe,
> And that which should accompany Old-Age,
> As Honor, Love, Obedience, Troopes of Friends,
> I must not looke to have. . . .
> (V, iii, 22–26)

In the same scene he insists upon putting on his armor, though " 'Tis not needed yet," and thus resumes the outward appearance proper to his nature, which is that of a soldier, not of a king. Macbeth no more than Mankynde can now regain renown and grace, but in Act V he resumes the virtues of a soldier and stands again as we first heard of him "lap't in proofe." It may be, as sentimental readers have held, that the otherwise curious attention given the praiseworthy death of young Seyward as Macbeth fights to the death offstage is meant to emphasize and to interpret this regeneration in the protagonist himself. "Gods Soldier be he. . . ." "They say he parted well, and paid his score, / And so God be with him." If these words

uttered just as Macduff reenters with Macbeth's head indeed apply
to the hero, then *Macbeth* does after all supply a trace of the argument of Mercy and Peace and of the Soul's lodgment at the right hand
of God.

The news of his wife's passing (V, v) elicits from Macbeth
immortal words close in spirit to Mankynde's reaction to the touch
of Death. If life leads to dusty death and signifies nothing, that is
as much as to say to dreary Death, "Dry is thy drift, dead is my
destiny." Each protagonist nonetheless continues to depend for a
while upon his false advisors. As he feels his mortality closing in
upon him, Mankynde looks up trustingly to the very figure who had
hired Coveytyse to ruin him. Unless the World, for old acquaintance,
helps him from this sorry chance, Mankynde pleads, he shall die.
Mundus is wonderfully sarcastic: "Owe, Mankynde, hathe Dethe
wyth the spoke?" Now Mankynde at last knows, and voices for the
audience, the truth that the World, with his agent Coveytyse, was
treacherous all along:

> HUMANUM GENUS. . . . He beryth a tenynge tungge.
>   Whyl I leyd wyth hym my lott
>   Ye seyn whou fayre he me behott;
>   And now he wolde I were a clott
>   In colde cley for to clynge.
> (ll. 2890–94)

None of the good men gathered round could miss the point that the
forces of evil speak fair but mean death.

Now Mundus takes away the last consolation of a worldly man.
As specified in the *nomina ludorum*, he has with him in addition to
his two servants in the first temptation play a Boy: "Mundus et cum
eo Voluptas, Stulticia, et Garcio."[12] The Proclamation adds a touch
of description of the Garcio. Mankynde, the flagbearer explains,
hopes that his goods shall be divided "amongis hys ny kynne,"

> But ther schal com a lythyr ladde wyth a torne hod,
>   I Wot Nevere Who schal by hys name, hys clothis be ful thynne,

Schal eryth the erytage that nevere was of hys blod,
Whanne al hys lyfe is lytyd upon a lytyl pynne.
(ll. 109–12)

Here Mundus bids the lad "aryse!" and confront Mankynde. I Wot
Nevere Who then hefts his stricken body and addresses him cruelly
and cryptically:

> Whou faryst, Mankynde? art thou ded?
>> Be Goddys body, so I wene.
>> He is hevyer thanne any led.
>> I wold he were gravyn undyr grene.
> HUMANUM GENUS. Abyde, I breyd uppe with myn hed.
>> What art thou? what woldyst thou mene?
>> Wheydyr comyst thou for good or qwed?
>
> . . . .
>
>> Fro whom comyst thou, good knave?
>> What dost thou here? what woldyst thou have?
>>> (ll. 2921–32)

When the Boy has told him, Mankynde is at last completely disabused. Bitterly he gives voice to what seems to him the illogic of
this disinheritance, while Garcio laughs in triumph: "Ya, ya, thi
parte schal be the leste. / Deye on, for I am maystyr here." Mankynde
has only to learn the Boy's name, which is no name at all.

The rest of Mankynde's part is lamentation. He says, "Now am
I sory of my lyf," but sheds no penitential tears. He has purchased
much and of his purchase, so he phrases it, he is woe. He regrets
that the unnamed "gelding" shall inherit it, instead of his own
"wyfe" and "chyldyr" (l. 2976), and he remembers now a verse
that David spake and finds it true: "Tesauriyat, et ignorat cui
congregabit ea" (Psalm 39.6). Before dying he makes explicit the
application of his experience—"For many men thus servyd be /
Thorwe the werld in dyverse place." His last word this side the grave
is mercy, but Anima, his Soul, has scant hope of it. Anima chastises
the body for yielding to its weaknesses, "And al it is for gyle." Malus

Angelus has won, and the last words of the Soul are to say that to have persevered in sin was madness:

> This devyl wyl have me away.
> Weleaway! I was ful wod
> That I forsoke myn Aungyl Good
> And with Coveytyse stod
> Tyl that day that I schuld dey.
> (ll. 3068–72)

Similarly, the empty prospect of old age and the sense that life is without meaning, "a Tale / Told by an Ideot," do not in themselves bring home to Macbeth the trickery of the Weird Sisters. He must be forcibly disabused. Not until word that Birnam Wood is moving does he begin "To doubt th'Equivocation of the Fiend, / That lies like truth" (V, v, 42–44). and still, slaying young Seyward and meeting the challenge of Macduff, he supposes that he bears "a charmed Life, which must not yeeld / To one of woman borne." Macduff's reply leaves him shaken and aware:

> Dispaire thy Charme,
> And let the Angell whom thou still hast serv'd
> Tell thee, Macduffe was from his Mothers womb
> Untimely ript.   (V, viii, 13–16)

Daunted momentarily by this last proof of infernal equivocation, Macbeth is nonetheless able to speak the truth of his predicament in a moral injunction as general as that of Mankynde:

> And be these Jugling Fiends no more beleev'd
> That palter with us in a double sence,
> That keepe the word of promise to our eare,
> And breake it to our hope.   (V, viii, 19–22)

The "us" and "our" are not kingly; they bespeak the tragic hero's bond with common humanity.

As an image on the stage, Mankynde's encounter with the Garcio resembles Macbeth's encounter with the crowned Child and the bloody Child in the witch's cavern (IV, i) much more closely than

it does his final encounter with Macduff. This is also true of the
meaning of the Garcio, symbolizing the future as the Child symbolizes
the descendants of Banquo, who shall inherit the crown that Macbeth has damned himself to get. Macbeth does not understand the
symbolism of these apparitions raised by Hecate. They themselves
make the equivocal promises about "none of woman borne" and
Birnam Wood, which he interprets to mean that he need not fear
mundane justice but "Shall live the Lease of Nature." He is naive
enough to ask, "Shall Banquo's issue ever / Reigne in this King-
dome?" A show of eight kings followed by Banquo is the answer,
and his strange reaction is to order the slaughter of Macduff's family:
"His Wife, his Babes, and all unfortunate Soules / That trace him
in his Line." ·It is as if, like Herod, by slaying all the innocents he
might slay the Child who was King. Much earlier, musing about
Banquo just before arranging the attempt to murder him and his child
Fleance, he had stated the equivalent truth to that which "I Wot
Nevere Who" brings home to Mankynde:

> They hayl'd him Father to a Line of Kings.
> Upon my Head they plac'd a fruitlesse Crown,
> And put a barren Scepter in my Gripe,
> Thence to be wrencht with an unlineall Hand,
> No Sonne of mine succeeding: if't be so,
> For *Banquo's* Issue have I fil'd my Minde,
> For them, the gracious *Duncan* have I murther'd,
> Put Rancours in the Vessell of my Peace
> Onely for them, and mine eternall Jewell
> Given to the common Enemie of Man,
> To make them Kings, the Seedes of *Banquo* Kings.
>
> (III, i, 60–70)

This is to say that the scene between Garcio and Mankynde finds its
Shakespearean equivalent earlier in the design; Macbeth's realization
that his dearly purchased crown shall go to strangers is not saved
until the last, and his last encounter is not with the symbolic Child
equivalent to the *Castell* playwright's Garcio.

And yet in a sense perhaps it is. Cleanth Brooks has indicated how the idea of the Child, bloody but triumphant, pervades *Macbeth*. Macbeth, in Brooks's phrase, wages war on children, but the Child, like Garcio frail with his thin clothes and torn hood, defeats him, is "maystyr here." Correspondingly, the Garcio may be glimpsed from time to time in the company of Mundus, so that the audience may wonder at his identity and meaning, which are not made fully clear till Mankynde's death. Mankynde himself is both newborn babe and young lad before he is king. And although one cannot attribute to the *Castell* playwright Shakespeare's esemplastic imagination, there is a notable frequency of children and boys in the language of the play, sometimes resulting in strikingly Macbethian images, that cannot be wholly attributed to the demands of bombast and alliteration. Thus Pride instructs Mankynde (l. 1052), "Bete boyes tyl they blede," and the boy appears threatening and martial in the first speech of Mundus (ll. 189–90): "What boy bedyth batayl or debaytyth with blad / Hym were betyr to ben hangyn hye in hell herne." Wrath remarks (l. 924): "Sum boy schal be betyn and browth undyr bonde." In *Macbeth* the image, with its mixture of weakness and strength, enters in the simile of the naked, newborn babe striding the blast. Aspects of it recur in Lady Macbeth's infant whose brains she would dash out, in Fleance, in "the Boy *Malcolme*" hailed king at the end of the tragedy, in Lady Macduff's defiant son, in the "Lilly-liver'd Boy" whom Macbeth bullies in Act V, scene iii, in young Seyward who appears only in the last scene to bid battle and debate with blade before being cut down by the tyrant. It bears a relation (explicit in the phrase "the Seedes of *Banquo*") to the recurrent imagery of seeds and plants in *Macbeth*, so that even the approach of Birnam Wood to Dunsinane is related to Macbeth's defeat by the Child. And finally, in Macduff who was "from his Mothers womb / Untimely ript," Macbeth faces the bloody Child grown up and triumphant and learns through him the last treachery of the instruments of darkness.

CHAPTER IV

Mankynde in Othello

—Nigra sum sed formosa.

In *Wisdom Who is Christ*, grace is conceived of as a marriage of Mankynde with Christ, "Wyffe of eche chose sowle" (l. 16), lovely and amiable "To be halysde and kyssyde of mankynde" (l. 44).[1] The mystical bond of love strengthens the mind, makes pure the soul, and bestows wisdom upon those perfect in it. "Wo takyt me to spowse, may veryly wene—" asserts Christ-Wisdom,

> Yff above all thynge ye love me specyall—
> That rest and tranqwyllyte he xall sene,
> And dey in sekyrnes of joy perpetuall.
> (ll. 57–60)

Already we encounter the vocabulary of *Othello*. Desdemona is Othello's "Soules Joy." Perdition will catch his soul, his words imply just as Iago begins to break their bond of love, when he loves her not, and chaos, a chaos of spiritual disorder, will come again. For "rest and tranqwyllyte" Othello has "Content" and the "Tranquill minde," to which he bids farewell during the temptation scene.

But a man is flawed. Made up of reason and sensuality, he may, so the exposition in *Wisdom* continues, act the part of angel or, practiced upon by the Fiend, of beast. The potential imperfection of all human nature is expressed through vesture by the black mantle upon the white cloth of gold of the Soul's costume as interpreted by Wisdom and by Anima's own allusion to Canticles I. 4–5:

> Nigra sum, sed formosa. . . .
> For this dyrke schadow I bere of humanyte,
> That as the tabernacull of cedar wythowt yt ys blake
> Ande wythine as the skyn of Salamone full of bewty.
> (ll. 164–68)

Wisdom explains (ll. 149–56) that the black stands for the Soul's capacity to sin at the prompting of "sensualyte," and white for its ability to know the deity through reason. Such emblematic use of black and white offers one of the play's most interesting points of contact with *Othello*, wherein for example the Duke remarks, just after Othello has sworn that passion shall not dull his "speculative, and offic'd Instrument," that is, his reason,

> If Vertue no delighted Beautie lacke,
> Your Son-in-law is farre more Faire then Blacke.
>> (I, iii, 290–91)

Shakespeare would hardly miss the opportunity to reinforce through visual effects the moral symbolism of white and black that pervades the language of *Othello*. The Othello of stage tradition is gowned during the early scenes in white. With his black hands and face visible, he is iconographically similar to the Soul in *Wisdom*, all white except for the black mantle. This "dark shadow" of the irrational and emotional forces in humanity equals the very "shadowing passion" in which Othello states that human nature has been instructed to "invest her selfe" in his case (IV, i, 40–42). Morocco in *The Merchant of Venice* (II, i), we may recall, is "a tawnie Moore all in white" whom Portia calls "as faire / As any commer I have look'd on yet," so that the image is ready to take on its moral symbolism when involved in the temptation plot.[2]

At the outset of both *Wisdom* and *Othello* black is aligned with the passionate forces in human nature that oppose virtue, in the one play called sensuality and in the other usually passion—though as we shall notice Iago speaks of "Sensualitie" in a scene that prepares for and helps interpret Othello's temptation. Most likely, the contrast of symbolic black and white expressed itself on Shakespeare's stage through visual effects as well as through language, as it does in the religious drama. The struggle of what Othello calls "blood" against man's judgment or "safer guides," deluded in the temptation scene by devil or demi-devil, underlies the tragedy as it does the moral drama. Each play initially presents a full portrait of a hero married to good who is in the differing specific terms of the two plays paradoxically weak and strong, baptismal and experienced, innocent and virtuous at once, and matched unknowingly against a single brilliant tempter.

The Lucifer of *Wisdom* exhibits a skill in specious argument worthy of the calumniator of Desdemona. Just as Christ-Wisdom had feared might happen, Lucifer presents evil suggestion to the mind of the protagonist, entices his understanding with it, and causes his free will to consent its "yll lessons to lere" (l. 303), yet all the while Mankynde thinks that he is talking to a well-meaning young man of the world and not to the Devil in this guise. Though the playwright drops the marriage metaphor during the phase of sin, Mankynde therein unwittingly betrays the holy spouse of his soul and makes her, Anima, turn as black and foul as he himself has become. In the scene of bitter peripeteia and anagnorisis in which he pivots back toward grace, the love metaphor is resumed. Othello too, though in the tragedy it is too late to make anything but tragic satisfaction, is permitted to shake free of the tempter's snare and regain his initial stature and appreciation of Desdemona in an analogous recognition scene—for which there is no hint in Cinthio's tale of the Moor of Venice. Wisdom offers to the Soul "this medsyne" (l. 970) of contrition, and Anima weeps as does Othello, whose eyes drop "teares as fast as the Arabian Trees / Their Medicinable gumme."

Before his temptation scene (III, iii), Shakespeare takes pains to establish the virtuous, susceptible innocence of the newly married Othello in Venice and, equally necessary to the design, to introduce properly the agent of evil suggestion. His purpose corresponds to that of the two opening stages in the outline of *Wisdom*. Othello is "fast married" to the play's representative of heavenly goodness, "the divine Desdemona," and what he says of his own spiritual condition is borne out: "My Parts, my Title, and my perfect Soule / Shall manifest me rightly" (I, ii, 31–32). His perfection of soul is chiefly manifested by the control of his reason over his passion just as Mankynde's is expressed more statically in terms of reason's dominance over "sensualite." Though capable of having his judgment "collied," blackened, by passion, Othello is presently a man whose reason controls him. His first words, " 'Tis better as it is," prefer restraint to violence, like his cool reception of the angry Brabantio and his men, "Keepe up your bright Swords, for the dew will rust them" (I, ii, 59)—while Iago tries to make a midnight street brawl out of the encounter. The round, unvarnished tale he tells the reverend signiors of Venice in defense of his elopement likewise illustrates unusual self-control and ability to remain calm in a difficult situation.

In various ways, including the symbolism of black versus white, the theme of passion versus reason is made explicit in the opening scenes of *Othello* as well as implicit in Othello's behavior. The Moor asks Heaven to vouch with him that he does not desire Desdemona's company in Cyprus

> To please the pallate of my Appetite:
> Nor to comply with heat the yong affects
> In me defunct, and proper satisfaction.
> But to be free, and bounteous to her minde.
> (I, iii, 263–66)

Nor will he let wantonness seel his "speculative and offic'd Instrument." She, though her elopement was a violent and stormy act, "saw Othello's visage in his mind" (I, iii, 253), not in his black face. It is a marriage of true minds in which sensuality has only its proper subordinate place. Presently Shakespeare, though in the context of a villainous speech, states the opposition abstractly in the very terms of the Wisdom who is Christ: "If the braine of our lives had not one Scale of Reason, to poize another of Sensualitie, the blood, and basenesse of our Natures would conduct us to most prepostrous Conclusions. But we have Reason to coole our raging Motions, our carnall Stings, or unbitted Lusts" (I, iii, 32–36). Iago, to be sure, does not know how to apply this truth. Yet his words do fit Othello himself, who is to exchange blessedness for sin as his blood gains mastery over his deluded mind in the temptation scene.

The equivalent frail virtue of Mankynde is presented by speeches of Wisdom, who is expositor as well as spouse, and through emblematic staging and costuming. Aided by his mystical tracts, and perhaps by fifteenth-century iconography of Christ as Wisdom, he builds up a complex opening tableau to represent the soul in grace.

It is not as in the *Castell* play the soul newly born. The maid Anima, soon joined by the five Wits and by Mynde, Wyll, and Understanding, kneeling before Wisdom declares that she has sought his love "Fro my yougthe" (l. 18), and in her speech at the close of this first phase of the plot (ll. 309–24) we glimpse the vicissitudes of that long quest. Mynde, too, has had a checkered career, not without "yerys and dayes" of sinfulness. But at present the soul of Man and its attendants and guides, long since cleared of the curse of Adam through Christ's suffering, form a blessed "symylytude" of God above, whom they may therefore best know through self-knowledge. The regal Wisdom who is Christ makes clear how frail is this state of grace, and so transparently foreshadows the future course of the action. Over her white gown Anima wears the mantle of black. "Blake, by sterynge of synne, that cummyth all day," Wisdom explains, which stirring is derived from man's sensuality. If *Wisdom* were tragedy, then sensuality, "this dyrke schadow I bere of humanyte," would be its hero's tragic flaw. The white represents reason, the opposite power of knowing the Deity: "Thus a sowle ys bothe fowlle and fayer." These particularities of costume replace the Bonus and Malus Angelus of the *Castell* play. They are equivalent to the later personified Sensualyte and Reason of Henry Medwall's temptation play *Nature* (ca. 1498). In the first scene of *Wisdom* it is somewhat as if the susceptible baptismal innocence of Mankynde in a full scope play had been superimposed upon the hard-won virtue which he had achieved before his second fall. We encounter at a moment of perfect spiritual union with Godhead and at the beginning of a crucial episode in his life a hero, still universally representative, who is already adult, with a past history.

Othello combines experience with innocence in the same way. He is well into the vale of years, and scenes ii and iii of Act I yield glimpses of his past life. This was not, like Mankynde's, intermixed with sins, yet from the perspective of the play it forms the indifferent background to his union with Desdemona, to the condition of joy in which he now dwells. The story of his adventures "even from my boyish days" (I, iii, 132) that captivated Desdemona recalls the Soul's quest "Fro my yougthe" for union with Christ. The services which he has done the Signory (to be recalled again when Othello resumes noble stature in Act V) are sufficient, he feels justly confident, to out-tongue Brabantio's complaints.

Yet in Othello this strength of experience fuses with a truly baptismal innocence and susceptibility. The play opens in the night, and in some respects it is as if Othello, like Mankynde in the full scope plays, were newly born this night into the play-world. Mankynde in the *Castell* play (l. 284), though already baptized, says that he was "born thys nyth in blody ble," and Man in Medwall's *Nature* is also brought "thys nyght" (l. 92) to the natural world. Both are promptly introduced to Mundus, the world. Othello is new-married, not new-born, this night, but exhibits an inexperience with Italian manners and society comparable to Mankynde's inexperience with all human life. He lived about nine months in Venice before marrying Desdemona, having led a soldier's life "Till now, some nine Moones wasted" (I, iii, 84). "And little of this great world can I speake," the same passage continues, "More then pertaines to Feats of Broiles, and Battaile."

His present bond to Desdemona, like that described between Mankynde and Christ in *Wisdom*, is both religious and susceptible, one of "Sanctimonie, and a fraile vow" Iago calls it (I, iii, 361) which his wit and all the tribe of Hell shall readily dissolve. To Iago's ear their harmony takes on overtones of that very contemplative Christian mysticism which infuses *Wisdom*: Othello, he tells Cassio, "hath devoted, and given up himselfe to the Contemplation, marke: and devotement of her parts and Graces" (II, iii, 321–23). In soliloquy a moment later Iago observes that "His Soule is so enfetter'd to her Love" that she may control him utterly. The example Shakespeare chooses is not accidental: she could win the Moor even "to renownce his Baptisme, / All Seales, and Simbols of redeemed sin."

In *Othello* and in *Wisdom* alike the protagonist's fall into sin is adumbrated in the portrait of his preliminary virtuous innocence. He falls from grace when reason yields to devilish suggestion and no longer guides him. In a passage independent of the known sources of *Wisdom*, but traditional in its explication of the *mysterium iniquitatis* (ll. 289–308), Wisdom warns Mankynde not to let sensual suggestion gain control over reason, for that is how "the clene soule" that "stondyth as a kynge" "dothe spyll." Man should try to keep his five wits unexposed to the sensual enticements of the World, the Flesh, and the Fiend, but if he fails to do so, he must by no means lend the "nether parte of resone," that more closely connected with the wits, to sensuality, and then the "over parte" will safely retain "fre domynacion" of his being.

> Wan suggestyon to the Mynde doth apere,
>   Wndyrstondynge, delyght not ye therin.
> Consent not, Wyll, yll lessons to lere,
>   Ande than suche steryngys be no syn.
>
> (ll. 301–4)

Intended to tell Mankynde what not to let happen to him in this worldly life, Wisdom's words are in fact a precise description of the psychology of the temptation scene to follow. Lucifer there offers Mynde what he calls unabashedly "my suggestyun," deludes him with it, and so captivates Understanding and gains Wyll's consent. In Mankynde's life in sin the playwright will dramatize the ascendancy of sensuality over reason in terms of wild and devilish revelry. "Ande ever be mery; let revell rowte!" (l. 505) cries Lucifer near the close of the temptation, and Mynde rhymes in a new vocabulary expressive of his unwittingly corrupted state: "Ya! ellys I beschrew my snowte." The "Dewyll me spede!" laughs Wyll, and "the Devyll is up," though the Mights have no knowledge that they have been ensnared by the Devil. In *Othello*, the protagonist's fall from grace is not itself directly dramatized in bacchanalian terms, but it is so adumbrated in the experience of Cassio, who, though Othello himself has urged, "Let's teach our selves that Honourable stop / Not to out-sport discretion" (II, iii, 2–3), loses his immortal part to the devil wine. This is to say that Mankynde's experience is not reenacted in *Othello* entirely by the Moor alone. Othello's lapse from reasonable to passionate is interpreted and broadened in its meaning proleptically by Cassio's lapse in Act II, scene iii. This is a function of the scene quite in addition to its use at a more practical level of plot of providing Iago the occasion for bringing Desdemona into a compromis-

ing relationship to Cassio and thereby facilitating the slander of Act
III, scene iii.

Through Cassio, Shakespeare stresses the possibility of rude
passion's overcoming reason more heavily than it is stressed in the
opening scene of *Wisdom*, although by less transparent means.
Though he has been advised not to outsport discretion, Cassio's
virtues are undermined by an agency to which he is especially susceptible, the "invisible spirit of Wine," and of which he declares (II,
iii, 284) "let us call thee Divell." He goes on, with reference to his
wounding of Montano, "It hath pleas'd the divell drunkennesse, to
give place to the divell wrath, one unperfectnesse, shewes me another
to make me frankly despise myself"—to which Iago replies, "Come,
you are too severe a Moraller." Cassio laments having lost "the immortal part of myselfe," and adds, "what remaines is bestiall" (l.
264). And the immortal part is not only reputation but soul. With
"joy, pleasance, revell [Lucifer's word] and applause," Cassio perceives, we "transforme our selves into Beasts. . . . To be now a
sensible man, by and by a Foole, and presently a Beast. Oh strange!
Every inordinate cup is unbless'd, and the Ingredient is a divell."

In this scene the human capacity for violence is matched against
judgment in a context unusually fraught, even for *Othello*, with
religious allusions. "Well: heaven's above all," remarks Cassio early
in the scene, for example, "and there be soules must be saved, and
there be soules must not be saved." It is at the end of this scene that
Iago mentions the Moor's "Baptisme" and the "Seales, and Simbols
of redeemed sin." The wealth of such allusions in the language of
the scene tends to reestablish the theme of reason versus unreasoned
feeling in its original dramatic frame. Reason's loss of control will
mean the soul's loss of grace. The progress from sensible man to
fool and beast that Cassio speaks of is that which the Moor is
presently to undertake in the temptation scene. Shakespeare there
puts it succinctly in an exclamation:

> Exchange me for a Goat,
> When I shall turne the businesse of my Soule

> To such exufflicate, and blow'd Surmises,
> Matching thy inference.   (III, iii, 180–83)

But even here in Act II the relevance to Othello himself of the language of reason and passion in their relationship to grace is directly implied when he enters and says in his anger at Cassio and Montano,

> Now by Heaven,
> My blood begins my safer Guides to rule
> And passion (having my best judgment collied)
> Assaies to leade the way.   (II, iii, 204–7)

It is just such an inversion of Othello's spiritual nature which Iago shall accomplish—in the medieval pattern of suggestion, sensual delectation, and consent—in the temptation scene.

The word *collied*, associating unreasoning feeling (in this instance anger) with blackness, and judgment thereby with black's opposite, whiteness or fairness, offers but one of many points in Acts I and II at which Shakespeare establishes the theme of reason versus emotion by the same symbolism of color that is so prominent in *Wisdom*. His evident preoccupation with black and white as moral emblems, as I have suggested, makes likely a corresponding intention to reinforce language with vesture, possibly also with other stage effects of darkness and light. Othello virtuous, we have observed, is called "more faire then Blacke" just as the Soul is visibly "nigra . . . sed formosa." The color scheme is keyed to the morality of sensuality and chastity as well as to race, however inappropriate the particular application, in its first, vivid appearance in the language of the play, Iago's cry to Brabantio, "Even now, now, very now, an old blacke Ram / Is tupping your white Ewe" (I, i, 88–89).

The white ewe Desdemona exhibits always that whiter skin "then Snow, / And smooth as Monumentall Alablaster" of which Othello speaks in the last scene before he kills her, and it is always appropriate to her moral nature. The language of black and white in its moral signification, however, creates images of her which move

in a visual pattern like that presented by the maiden Anima in
Wisdom, who is first gowned in white, reappears all blackened and
foul to show graphically what Mankynde has done to his soul, and is
then restored to the purity of white after Mankynde's recognition and
contrition. When first deluded by Iago, Othello thinks that her
name "that was as fresh / As Dians Visage, is now begrim'd and
blacke / As mine own face" (III, iii, 386–88). Iago, as he promised
himself (II, iii, 366), has turned her virtue into pitch. Upon this
"faire Paper" (IV, ii, 71–72) has been written "Whore." As in the
"old fond Paradoxes" with which Iago earlier entertained Desdemona
(II, i, 130ff.), fairness has come to denote only outward, bodily
beauty, the wit or wisdom of woman being only for sensual (black
or foul) purposes. To Othello's deluded eye Desdemona has become
by the end of the temptation scene "the faire Divell," outwardly
white but black within. Of course it is only to Othello's eye that she
has changed; the real change is in his own mind. The language of
lust applied to her is a way of showing that the judgment of
Othello, who is eaten up with passion, has been collied. The defile-
ment of Desdemona, like that of Anima, is a projection of the defile-
ment of the mind of the protagonist. She is blackened nominally, just
as the courtesan Bianca is only nominally white. Thus Shakespeare's
use of the black-white antithesis runs parallel to that in the language
and stage effects of *Wisdom.*

Like the protagonist of *Wisdom*, then, Othello at the outset is fast
married to the play's embodiment of goodness. As Iago says, the
relationship is a kind of contemplation of her parts and graces. It is
analogous to the contemplative union with Christ which is the
mystical ideal of the author of *Wisdom*. It is intellectual before it
is physical, a marriage of true minds, for Desdemona "saw Othello's
visage in his mind" (I, iii, 253) not in his black face, and he would
have her with him at Cyprus not to please his sensual appetite, "But
to be free, and bounteous to her minde" (l. 266). The over-part of
reason rules the lower, which is in contact with the senses. She is his
"Soules Joy"—just as Christ is Anima's. He says so in conjunction
with an image that measures how far "hell's from Heaven." Like
Anima, the same passage continues (II, i, 186ff.), his "Soule hath

her content so absolute" that such another cannot follow in the unknown future. Their kisses are the greatest discords between them. In the secular terms at the core of the tragedy, she is the mainstay of all that is rational, loving, and noble in Othello. While he does not love her, "Chaos is come againe." Faith in her is dramatically equivalent to Mankynde's faith in Christ: it is the bond that diabolic temptation causes him to shatter and that recognition and penance enable him to reestablish.

The logic of temptation requires not only an initial state of susceptible grace and of innocence or virtue but some agent of evil suggestion. *Wisdom* neatly fulfills this requirement in its second scene, before proceeding efficiently to the temptation itself. In *Othello*, Shakespeare meets the same need, not quite with the same schematic efficiency, by introducing Iago in Act I, scene i, apart from the Moor and in company of a dupe to whom he will speak openly of his hatred of the general, and then by isolating Iago for three soliloquies that complete and deepen the first impression. The motives and strategy of Lucifer more nearly resemble Iago's than do those of any intermediate tempter.[3]

His adaptation of Lucifer to the role of tempter of Mankynde is a happy achievement of the playwright of *Wisdom*. Even the hostile critic Thomas Sharp in 1835, who thought the rest of the play rendered dull by religion, found "indications of a master hand" in the Lucifer scenes.[4] The master hand integrates the scene introducing Lucifer with the temptation scene itself in a way only approximated in the older *Castell* play. He is the first to introduce the nature and essential strategy of the tempter in a scene that along with his characterization of the protagonist in grace efficiently prepares for the temptation proper as in several Tudor interludes and in *Othello*. To deceive Mankynde he employs for the first time a spirit who is not in any sense part of Mankynde, and he is first to make of it a truly moral deception by which the mind of the hero mistakes evil for good and so engages the will and understanding in unwittingly wronging the play's representative of goodness and blackening the hero's soul.

Lucifer's motive is simple envy of the new creature that has been given the place he once occupied himself and would like to occupy again:

> Owt harow I rore
> For envy I lore.
> My place to restore
> God hath mad a man.
>
> (ll. 325–28)

"Presumynge in Godys syght" he was cast into Hell and Man replaced him:

> In reformynge of my place ys dyght
> Man, whom I have in most dyspyght,
> Ever castynge me with hem to fyght
> In that hewynly place he xulde not dwell.
>
> (ll. 337–40)

He is "as wyly now as than" and knows "all compleccions of a man, / Werto he ys most dysposyde" (ll. 341–44). He will delude Man's mind by "fals conjecture; / Yff he tende my reporture / I xall brynge hym to nought" (ll. 354–56). To the mind he shall "mak suggestyun," bring delectation to the understanding, and so gain the consent of the will. Since his true appearance is frightening, he will assume a pleasant disguise—that of what the stage direction calls "a goodly galont," a well-dressed man of the world.

> I wyll change me into bryghtnes,
>   And so hym to-begyle,
> Sen I xall schew hym perfyghtnes,
> And wertu prove yt wykkydnes;
> Thus wndyr colors all thynge perverse;
>   I xall never rest tyll the Soule I defyle.
>
> (ll. 375–80)[5]

Shakespeare similarly takes care, along with depicting his hero controlled by reason and suspended in grace by sanctimony and a frail vow, to introduce properly the play's agent of evil suggestion. Like Lucifer entering to the echoing strains of the hymn *tota pulcra es*, Iago shall, as he mutters in an aside (II, i, 202), "set downe the peggs that make this Musicke" between Othello and the object of his loving contemplation. Iago is a crux in Shakespeare criticism, but seen from the point of view of the theological drama that most nearly matches *Othello*, he becomes very clearly a devil in the form— not merely the garb but the body and to an extent the psychology— of an "honest" man. Compare with the language of Lucifer this comment of Iago just after he has noted how "His Soule is so enfetter'd to her Love" that Desdemona may "play the God" and "make, unmake, do what she list" to Othello, even were it to renounce baptism and the signs and symbols of redeemed sin:

> Divinitie of hell,
> When divels will the blackest sinnes put on,
> They do suggest at first with heavenly shewes,
> As I do now.

Making her virtuous appeal for Cassio seem to be lust, he declares, "So will I turne her vertue into pitch. . ." (II, iii, 356–66). "Suggest" is Lucifer's word, and the heavenly show is equivalent to Lucifer's "shew hym perfyghtnes." Shakespeare's tempter will again prove virtue wickedness. And when Iago turns her virtue into pitch (which defiles) the transformation will not of course be in Desdemona, who remains unchanged, but in the soul of the protagonist.

Othello's penetrating question near the close of the play, though it goes unanswered and may be unanswerable, defines Iago and his role in the tragedy in words that are both unambiguous and consistent with what we learn of Iago in Acts I and II: "Will you, I pray, demand that demy-Divell, / Why he hath thus ensnar'd my Soule and Body?" (V, ii, 301–2). We have seen a few lines earlier that Iago when wounded bleeds like a man, but, like a devil, is "not kill'd." At the outset he is made to hint at his dramatic origin in his complaint to Brabantio (I, i, 108–10): "Sir: you are one of those that will not serve God, if the devill bid you." The bond between the Moor and Desdemona, he is confident (I, iii, 363–64), will "be not too hard for my wits, and all the Tribe of hell." (The Lucifer of *Wisdom* vows [l. 372] "to all the dewllys of helle" to subvert

Mankynde.) If Iago's devilish side is implicit under cover of metaphor, as in Othello's question, his human side is obvious at a glance. Besides, he has a wife, a need for money, and his share of human doubts and dissatisfactions. His literary type is declared not through metaphor but dramatic irony, as in Brabantio's "Prophane wretch" and "villain" and Emilia's hypothesis that the slander was devised by

> some eternall Villaine,
> Some busie and insinuating Rogue,
> Some cogging, cozening Slave, to get some Office.
> (IV, ii, 130–32)

To which Iago replies truly, "Fie, there is no such man: it is impossible."

The first scene of *Othello*, besides its functions of rousing Brabantio and introducing the minor dupe Roderigo, serves like the second scene of *Wisdom* to lay bare the nature and essential strategy of the figure who will later beguile the protagonist in a temptation scene. Iago exhibits two qualities which define the character of Lucifer, hatred arising out of envy for a "place" and ability to operate under a goodly exterior: "by the faith of man / I know my price, I am worth no worsse a place" (I, i, 10–11). So Lucifer loured for envy because "my place to restore, / God hath mad a man" and despised Man for being set up in the "reformynge of my place." Iago further professes himself one of those "trym'd in Formes, and visages of Dutie" who throw "but showes of Service on their Lords" and so thrive by them. "Heaven is my Judge," he remarks with the trace of irony of all the religious references in the play, "not I for love and dutie / But seeming so, for my peculiar end" (I, i, 59–60). His pose of concerned counselor matches that of Lucifer's goodly gallant so alarmed at Mankynde's imperceptiveness. His second, most demi-devilish soliloquy (II, iii, 342–68) coming just after the initial portrait of Othello and not long before the temptation, best corresponds to Lucifer's self-introductory monologue delivered in his devil's array at the same point in the plot.

To define Iago's "peculiar end" is the major difficulty in under-

standing him, but it would seem to lie implicit in his charge to
Roderigo: "poyson his delight. . . . Though that his Joy be Joy, /
Yet throw such chances of vexation on't, / As it may loose some
colour" (I, i, 68–73). To do that to Mankynde in envy because
God made him and placed him in grace was Lucifer's motive.
Though in the Devil's role, Iago as a human personality cannot
hate Othello for that reason. To launch the action Shakespeare
grounds the hatred in something the Moor has done, namely,
promote Cassio over Iago to the lieutenancy. But despite later re-
minders of it this motive is obscured by others: that Iago is jealous of
Othello over Desdemona, that perhaps Othello has slept with Emilia,
that (nearer the truth one suspects) Cassio "hath a dayly beauty in
his life, / That makes me ugly" (V, i, 19–20). It would be in
character for Iago to express such envy of the daily beauty of Desdemona and Othello and of the harmony of their union. To Othello's
crucial question Iago will say nothing to add to what the Moor
already knows, which is only that Iago slandered Desdemona and
Cassio and so ensnared him body and soul. For Iago to speak and,
as any other villain would, to list his complaints for the bitter
satisfaction of it would be to disintegrate his hybrid nature by im-
plying that these human reasons were adequate to explain the energy
and persistence of his attack upon Othello's joy and all human
joy. The other, Luciferian motive he cannot restate because it is not
translatable into any human motive. To quiet the censor in us that
asks that a villain shall have some mundane reason for his actions
Shakespeare supplies token reasons, which reduce to envy.

The temptation scene in *Wisdom* (ll. 381–550) is made vividly
dramatic by the brilliant sophistry—what Lucifer calls "fals conjecture" and "reporture"—by which he beguiles the Mynde. It is
also strangely inconsistent within itself and with the opening depiction of Mankynde in grace, transitional to the plane of realism on
which the phase of sin is conducted. Mynde, Understanding, and
Wyll are still, to judge from their speeches, parts of the soul of the
human individual. So Lucifer spoke of them in anticipation of the
temptation: "In the soule ben thre partyes iwys," which he shall approach successively. "To the Mynde of the Soule I xall mak sug-

gestyun . . ." and so forth. Afterward he exults in having severed
from grace "the Soule" and "mankyn," always in the singular.
Presumably then the three "Mights" are still attired in the emblematic
white cloth of gold of the symbolic opening scene, though there
has been time for a costume change during the introduction of
Lucifer and though indeed it could be argued that the playwright
ordered scenes i and ii as he did so as to provide such time. Lucifer
however appears as the realistic "goodly galont," addresses the trio as
"Ye fonnyde fathers," and urges them to abandon their contemplative lives for the *vita mixta,* a clever euphemism here for the
life of sin, and in so doing to change their long dress. They become
in the next phase of the action three distinct human sinners. Either,
as is quite possible, the dramatist in his inexperience has lost control,
or else these middle stages of the plot are to be understood parabolical-
ly. He has not inadvertently forgotten the symbolic play-world in
which he began, for he forcibly returns us and the multiple protagonist to it in the recognition scene. Lucifer does not, at any rate, explicitly seek to break up the mystical union of Mankynde and
Christ-Wisdom which was impressed upon us at the outset. Because
the playwright draws so heavily upon his source in Hilton's *Epistle
on Mixed Life,* when Lucifer does refer to Christ it is only as the
supreme example and the very inventor of the *vita mixta.* Of Christ
as spouse of each chosen soul there is no mention, as if the author
had indeed forgotten or was the plaything of his sources. Yet it is
as a violation of Mankynde's love for Christ-Wisdom that we are
to understand the surrender of the composite central figure, at least
in retrospect, for that is how Wisdom afterward describes it.

Whatever we make of the shift in dramatic mode in *Wisdom,* it
means that the phases of temptation and especially of sin do not
resemble the corresponding phases of *Othello* as they would if the
playwright had remained on the level of theological symbolism. Still,
the scenes are broadly equivalent. The course of evil is made to seem
that of good. The mind deluded, reason yields its control to sensuality or passion. The perfect spiritual union of the protagonist with
the play's objectification of goodness in his world is broken in a
single scene. The three voices of Mankynde speak, before they see

the goodly gallant, of their devotion to Jesu; he "enduyde ws wyth wertu," "wyth feyth ws dyd renew," and "made ws hys creaturys so specyally." Othello's comment at the head of the temptation proper (though he is already troubled by the guilty light in which Iago has cast the harmless business between Desdemona and Cassio) carries similar force:

> Excellent wretch: Perdition catch my Soule
> But I do love thee: and when I love thee not,
> Chaos is come againe.   (III, iii, 90–92)

The implication is that when the bond of love is broken, as it is by the close of the scene, Othello's spiritual condition will return to disorder and his soul be damnable. Such is the allegorical meaning of the temptation in *Wisdom*. Lucifer engages Mynde by employing his ability to quote Scripture (Matthew 20.6), "quid hic statis tota die ociosi?" And he adds the gloss: "The Dewyll hath acumberyde yow expres" (ll. 394–96). Mynde counters: "He ys not ydyll that wyth Gode ys," and the Devil at once offers his proof ("thys ys my suggestyun"), namely the argument from Hilton. If a man has wife, children, and other charges and gives himself wholly to prayer and ease of body so that his charges perish, then he can hardly claim that he is with God. Martha, after all, was not unpleasing to God. Mynde can still object that Mary pleased him more and, somewhat more feebly, that "Contemplatyff lyff is sett befor." But Martha, the insidious argument runs, received eternall bliss, which is enough, and, conclusively, Christ himself was never, as the Mynde must grant, a contemplative, but as an example to man spoke with sinners and holy people, both labored and prayed, and in short initiated the *vita mixta.*

By this accurate description of the life of Christ, rather than by the calumniation that we might have expected after scene i, Lucifer drives deeper the wedge that he has introduced between the Mynde and Christ. We must assume the description to be just, for it is taken from Hilton, one of the founders of the school of mysticism to which the playwright manifestly belongs. To W. K. Smart, who believes that Mynde is a monk, the fallacy in Lucifer's argument lies in applying it to the small class of men dedicated to contemplation.[6] But if Mynde is the Mynde of Mankynde, Lucifer's reasoning is not so easy to refute. Mynde himself is troubled: "I kan not belewe thys ys trew" (l. 430). Lucifer allows him no time to think. There is dread in the contemplative life, he adds immediately, though not quite consistently, because all the fasting, waking, praying, hard living and discipline, weeping, silence and eschewing of surfeits are difficult to perform, and men who fail "offende Gode hyghly." Moreover, their bodies wasted and their wits grown feeble, some fall to despair and some to madness; and know it well, "God is not plesyd with thys." So Mankynde should leave this lonely life, be in the world, use its necessities; common life is best, for, as if there were presumption in being a contemplative, "Who clymyt hye, hys fall gret ys" (l. 444). Lucifer has gained domination over Mynde:

> MYNDE. Truly, me seme ye have reson.
> LUCYFER. Aplye yow then to this conclusyun.
> MYNDE. I kan make no replicacyon,
> 　　　Your resons be grete.
> 　　I kan not forgett this informacyon.
> LUCYFER. Thynke therwppon, yt ys yowr salvacyon.
> 　　　　　　　　(ll. 445–50)

The deception is yet more clever than Smart would have it. We may be sure that what Mynde is invited to think upon will involve damnation, not salvation, yet what "replicacyon" can be made? The Devil has spoken what are, on the whole, a series of truths, and if it be granted that Mynde is not a monk or other professional contemplative, it would seem these truths should be applied in his life. As Lucifer turns to Mankynde's Understanding and Wyll, to whom he now has access, we discover that the principle of his trickery is semantic. The meaning of "mixed life" shifts subtly from the good life partly active, partly contemplative, to a life of spiritual disorder, of sin. The one kind of worldliness becomes the other.

Lucifer speaks now to the Understanding of riches, lust, and liking, and gets the predictable reply: "In thys I fele in manere of dylectacyon" (l. 462). "A, ha, ser!" Lucifer cries,

then ther make a pawsacyon.
Se and beholde the worlde abowte.
Lytyll thynge suffysyt to salvascyon;
All maner synnys dystroyt contryscyon.

(ll. 463–66)

He advises Wyll to leave his studies, prayers, and penance (the mark of hypocrites), to consider that there is no sin in meat, health, wine, riches, and fine clothes, and to leave his nice chastity and take a wife—"Bettur ys fayer frut than fowll pollucyon. / What seyth sensualite to this conclusyon?" (ll. 477–78). Wyll freely consents to what the audience, with its advantage of knowing the true identity of the tempter, may perceive through the rationalizing to be all manner of sins, a life of sensuality and, as the recognition scene will later stress, the very "fowll pollucyon" of spirit which Lucifer here imputes to the contemplative life. The transformation in the protagonist, later to be manifest in his dress and disorderliness, is apparent even during the temptation in his very language. "Ya," sneers Wyll, "I woll no more row ageyn the floode" (l. 491). Mynde rhymes Lucifer's injunction "let revell rowte!" with a line yet more expressive of corruption: "Ya, ellys I beschrew my snowte!" (l. 506). And Understanding echoes it: "And yff I care, cache I the gowte!" As the deluded central figures scamper from the stage Wyll, who is last, cries to the audience with unwitting irony, "Farwell . . . , the Dewyll ys wppe!"

Lest the audience miss the point of what they have witnessed, Lucifer is granted four stanzas of exultation before he departs from the play. "Resone," he declares, "I have made both deff and dumme; / Grace ys owt and put arome." That incomparable Soul that God made in his own likeness will soon be most reprovable, in the likeness rather of a fiend of Hell. He muses finally upon the change he has wrought. While Mankynde is pure,

Verely, the soule God ys wythin;
Ande wen yt ys in dedly synne,
Yt ys werely the Develys place.

> Thus by colours and false gynne
> Many a soule to hell I wyn. (ll. 544–48)

Iago often generalizes in similar accents. Compare his comment during Othello's fit (IV, i, 46–48): "Thus credulous Fooles are caught, / And many worthy, and chast Dames even thus, / (All guiltlesse) meete reproach."

Iago achieves in the single scene of temptation in *Othello* an equivalent transformation in the protagonist by analogous means. At the start, Othello is bound in love to Desdemona, to the "devotement of her parts and Graces," his content absolute; at the end he is in spirit wholly alienated from her. His reason is beguiled, he has bid farewell to "the Tranquill minde" and to content and become, as his tempter accurately notes, "eaten up with Passion." Blood rules over judgment, and his speech has revealingly turned violent, incoherent, and bestial after the "Othello music" of Acts I and II. The change has been wrought under cover of the goodly exterior of a twenty-eight-year-old seemingly "full of Love, and Honestie" whom Shakespeare's audience would by this time have identified as part devil and who suggests wickedness, as devils will, "at first with heavenly shewes." Indeed, Iago takes virtue and more directly "prove[s] yt wykkydnes" so to beguile the protagonist than does Lucifer himself. There are three lines of calumny in Lucifer's temptation:

> But trust not thes prechors, for they be not goode,
> For they flatter and lye as they wore woode;
> Ther ys a wolffe in a lombys skyn.
>
> > (ll. 488–90)

These ironic lines calling attention to Lucifer's own technique (and incidentally arguing against Smart's conviction that the tempted are monks) anticipate Titivillus' more central slander of the good priest Mercy in *Mankind*, but they are only parenthetical. Lucifer so to speak slanders the contemplative life by showing it to be displeasing to God and by associating it with pride and "fowll pollucyon." Iago makes the divine Desdemona by her very goodness seem corrupt and damnable. He turns her virtue into pitch. He undoes "her Credite with the Moore" and makes violence against her and the good Cassio seem to accord with the will of God.

Iago's powers of evil inference are by far greater than Lucifer's. They are gestic as well as logical and verbal, as we may glimpse in Othello's description of Iago's manner early in the scene:

> And when I told thee, he was of my Counsaile,
> Of my whole course of wooing; thou cried'st, Indeede?
> And didd'st contract, and purse thy brow together,
> As if thou then hadd'st shut up in thy Braine
> Some horrible Conceite.   (III, iii, 111–15)

Rather than always spelling out his misdirections, he can make Othello first beg for them and then conceive them independently. The literal terms of the mental struggle are sexual rather than Christian as in *Wisdom*, the contrast being the sharper since the *Wisdom* playwright for a time deviates from his metaphor of love and marriage.

Still, Iago's temptation of Othello may be regarded as parallel to Lucifer's of Mankynde, even in its progress from rational or intellectual to more sensual proofs once the mind has been engaged and partly won over to folly. Iago begins by speaking facts and philosophical truths. Cassio was of Othello's counsel in the wooing. "Men should be what they seeme"—words spoken by a tempter who is not what he is carry the same irony as Lucifer's in reference to the wolves in lamb's clothing. Unclean apprehensions may creep into the purest breast. It is Iago's nature to shape "faults that are not," and it would be better if Othello's wisdom took no notice. "Goode name in Man & woman (deere my Lord) / Is the immediate Jewell of their Soules. . . ." A man should beware of jealousy, which tortures him who suspects yet fondly loves.

Othello's response to this last discloses for the first time in the scene his awakening propensity for violence toward Desdemona:

No: to be once in doubt,
Is to be [once] resolv'd: Exchange me for a Goat,
When I shall turne the businesse of my Soule
To such exufflicate, and blow'd Surmises,
Matching thy inference.   (III, iii, 179–83)

He will not suspect her because of her sociableness nor his weak merits; he requires proof. "And on the proofe, there is no more but this, / Away at once with Love, or Jealousie." The passion implicit in this response emboldens Iago further to direct the business of Othello's soul toward violence with inferences based on statements that an uncorrupted mind would question or reject as irrelevant: Venetian women are secretly unfaithful.

She did deceive her Father, marrying you,
And when she seem'd to shake, and feare your lookes,
She lov'd them most.

But Othello can only reply "Dost thou say so?" and "And so she did." He is, as Iago twice calls to attention, "mov'd," so much so that Iago may risk a line of argument that a few moments earlier would perhaps have got him taken by the throat and smitten to death like that base Judean who traduced the state: her will must be foul, for, consider, she married a Moor! Othello's puzzled reason cannot supply the obvious retort, that she saw Othello's visage in his mind, that theirs was a marriage of true minds. Yet, as he glimpses her a few lines later, he can still resist Iago's inference and echo with Shakespearean eloquence the words of Mankynde at the same stage of the temptation. Mankynde had simply said, "I kan not belewe thys ys trew" (l. 430). Compare Othello: "If she be false, Heaven mock'[s] it selfe: / Ile not beleeve't" (III, iii, 278–79). Othello's mind has nonetheless accepted the suggestion that his love's a whore. Just as Lucifer at this point could reach the Understanding with sensual suggestion rather than the rational inference by which originally he tempted the Mynde, Iago calls up vivid images of Cassio with Desdemona. The shift from rational to sensuous false proofs is accomplished in language charged with overtones of theology:

> Give me the Occular proofe,
> Or by the worth of mine eternall Soule,
> Thou had'st bin better have bin borne a Dog
> Then answer my wak'd wrath. . . .
> If thou dost slander her, and torture me,
> Never pray more: Abandon all remorse.
> On Horrors head, Horrors accumulate:
> Do deedes to make Heaven weepe, all Earth amaz'd:
> For nothing canst thou to damnation adde,
> Greater then that.
>
> IAGO.   O Grace! O Heaven forgive me!
> Are you a Man? Have you a Soule? or Sense?
> God buy you: take mine Office.
>
>   (III, iii, 360–75)

Thus the atmosphere in which Othello's spirit is alienated from Desdemona recalls the issue originally central in such scenes in English drama, Man's soul's damnation or redemption.

Iago quickly summons the provocative image of Othello grossly gaping on to "Behold her top'd." "Death, and damnation. Oh!" Othello roars. Actually to catch them in flagrante delicto were of course impossible, even if they were "as prime as Goates, as hot as Monkeyes, / As salt as Wolves in pride" or as gross as (like Cassio) "Ignorance, made drunke," but lately (on a night that never was nor could have been) Iago lay with Cassio who dreamed he was with Desdemona and whispered:

> Let us be wary, let us hide our Loves,
> And then (Sir) would he gripe, and wring my hand:
> Cry, oh sweet Creature: then kisse me hard,
> As if he pluck't up kisses by the rootes,
> That grew upon my lippes, laid his Leg ore my Thigh,
> And sigh, and kisse, . . .   (III, iii, 420–25)

Othello understands this to denote a foregone conclusion. Finally Iago conjures up the false vision of Cassio with the handkerchief, which in fact resides at this moment in the villain's pocket:

> such a Handerchiefe
> (I am sure it was your wives) did I to day
> See Cassio wipe his Beard with.
>
> (III, iii, 437–39)

To the jealous, as Iago remarked to himself a few lines earlier in the scene, mere trifles are "confirmations strong, / As proofes of holy Writ." The violent and passionate sub-nature of the protagonist now dominates his judgment, and in this disfigured state of soul he commits himself in what he thinks is a sacred vow to desecrate Desdemona: "Yeeld up (O Love) thy Crowne, and hearted Throne / To tyrannous Hate" (III, iii, 447–48).

The phase of *Wisdom* dramatizing sin offers the play's extreme deviation from the symbolic mode of representation established in scene i and reestablished in scene v. The terms are those of local and topical satire. Mynde, Understanding, and Wyll, hitherto parts of the soul, become three individualized men, realistically dressed as gallants about town, who specialize, so they tell us, in maintenance, perjury, and lechery respectively, and who during the ballet sequence shade into personifications of these social vices. Corresponding to this shift in mode, Wisdom is absent and unmentioned. Lucifer is missing too, despite his promise in his speech of exultation (ll. 519–50) that he would stay on to steer Mankynde in sinfulness.

Although the correspondences to *Othello* are not sufficient to warrant close comparison, they still supply certain new angles of insight. One common aspect of *Wisdom* and *Othello* now comes into prominence: that in each three men are misled by the devil-figure. In a sense, we realize, *Othello* too has a multiple protagonist. There are not matching pairs. We cannot link Othello's disorderliness nor misguided sense of justice to Mynde's graft, and Cassio's weaknesses with Understanding's new fondness for perjury, even though Wyll in his lechery makes an interesting counterpart to Roderigo. But one implication is worth pursuing a little distance, namely that Iago's effect upon Cassio and Roderigo helps express the nature of Othello's transgression itself. Lucifer told Mankynde "ever be mery; let revell rowte!" We have seen already that Cassio's drunkenness and the "foule Rout" that it leads to comment in advance upon the fall of Othello from the path of reason. Cassio falls in a scene (II, iii) fairly bristling with echoes of the theology of *Wisdom*, of souls saved and lost, of devils, love and "Contemplation," and midway in the scene Othello enters to say with unwitting prescience that blood and passion begin to get the better of his judgment. Othello in Act IV, after Iago "Hath pudled his cleare Spirit," is in a state of disorder analogous, we are given to understand, to the state of "revell and applause" to which the Devil wine brings Michael Cassio.

After Othello has fallen under Iago's spell, we discover that Cassio, originally described as "A Fellow almost damn'd in a faire Wife," has a mistress who is a common harlot, and Bianca makes her three appearances. Bianca is of course the projection of what Othello now thinks Desdemona to be, but beyond that she and Cassio in his relationship to her, like the dance of "harlottys" in *Wisdom* (l. 760), tell us something of the spiritual condition of the protagonist. That is not lust, but like drunkenness it is a spiritual disorder akin to lust in its subjection of reason to sensuality or passion. Bianca's and Cassio's relationship is inharmonious. At their first meeting in the play Bianca suspects Cassio with some "newer Friend," and he tells her to throw her "vilde gestes in the Divels teeth, / From whence you have them. You are jealious now . . ." (III, iv, 184–85). Then, in the next scene, Othello, wrought to incoherence by Iago's seamy picturing of Desdemona "naked with her Friend in bed" and of Cassio "With her? On her: what you will," marks Cassio's "Fleeres, the Gybes, and notable Scornes / That dwell in every Region of his face" as he talks of Bianca and briefly squabbles with her once more. It is uncharacteristic behavior for the lieutenant who "hath a dayly beauty in his life," and I think that beyond its function in confirming Othello's will to murder Desdemona it also comments upon Othello's own disfigurement.

As the scene (IV, i) continues, Othello strikes Desdemona, calling her "Divell," and stalks from the stage muttering incoherently of "Goates and Monkeys." This behavior, as Lodovico's choric comment emphasizes, is that of passion free from the control of judgment:

> Is this the Noble Moore, whom our full Senate
> Call all in all sufficient? Is this the Nature
> Whom Passion could not shake? Whose solid vertue
> The shot of Accident, nor dart of Chance,
> Could neither graze, nor pierce?
>
> (IV, i, 275–79)

He is, as Iago drily adds, "much chang'd" from the Othello of Acts
I and II. And language, as in *Wisdom* (and certain of the Tudor
interludes intervening), is a key to the manner of the change.
"Goates and Monkeys" is the language of sensuality, of lechery; it
is Iago's language from the temptation scene—"Were they as
prime as Goates, as hot as Monkeyes," not, again, that Othello is
lecherous but that his condition is such a state of moral inversion of
the faculties as lechery is. Language is the reflection of spirit, and his
language as G. Wilson Knight has said, now chaotic, hellish, and
ugly, is opposite to the music of Othello uncorrupted.[7] He sees "that
nose" of Cassio's (IV, i, 146) but not "that dogge" he shall throw
it to. Earlier in the scene (ll. 42ff.), just as he collapses into a trance
(which is not "an Epilepsie" in the usual sense, as Iago claims, but a
paralysis of the guiding faculties from the working of Iago's medi-
cine) he mutters "(pish) Noses, Eares, and Lippes: is't possible.
Confesse? Handkerchiefe? O divell." It is a long way back from this
to *Wisdom's* "Ya! ellys I beschrew my snowte" (l. 506), but the
technique for revealing a change of inner nature is the same. The
epithets which Othello directs to Desdemona—"Devill," "lewde
Minx," and so forth—tell us nothing about her, everything about
him; it is he who is bedevilled, lewd, and bestial. The "sweating
Divell heere / That commonly rebels" (III, iv, 42–43) is not in
Desdemona's palm but Othello's mind, symbol and symptom of the
rebellion within him. Truly Iago has turned Othello's wit the seamy
side out and made us witness to that side.

Roderigo, the poor embodiment of that mere "Lust of the blood,
and . . . permission of the will" which may substitute for love, is the
clear equivalent to Wyll, also called Lechery in this phase of *Wisdom*,
who becomes during the life-in-sin a separate individual as well as

faculty of Mankynde and, briefly, the personification of his special vice. Indeed, the scheme by which Iago proposes to clear the way to Desdemona by having them conspire to dispose of Cassio, not, to be sure, by throwing him into the Marshalsea but simply by "knocking out his braines" (IV, ii, 236), is of the same family as that by which Wyll hopes to get rid of Janet's husband. And in the scene in which the scheme is put into effect (V, i), Shakespeare for the only time in the tragedy brings together with Iago the three "credulous Fooles" whom Iago controls.

From the point of view of *Wisdom* we can see the meaning of his doing so. It is, we know, "betweene twelve and one," the same odd-even time of night in which the play began, and it is a scene full of noise, violence, and discord. Othello merely walks across the stage, remaining for an interval of only ten lines. But it is directly from here, saying "Strumpet I come" (V, i, 34) that Othello goes to murder Desdemona, and the disharmony of the scene is transferred to, and comments upon, that mission. Cassio, just before Othello's entrance, is thrust in the leg by Roderigo and wounds him in return. Iago murders him in the dark. Cassio lies bleeding, his leg cut in two as he thinks, with Bianca blubbering over him. "This is the fruits of whoring," Iago piously remarks, as he instinctively tries to implicate her. Ironically, he also tells Emilia to run to the citadel to inform their lord and lady and so himself provides the agency of Othello's tragic recognition.

The recognition scene in *Wisdom* is the most theatrically effective and powerfully imagined part of the play. Just as the three sinners have cleared the way for Wyll's lust by their plan to get rid of her husband (by terrifying him "Tyll he leve that jelousy" or throwing him unjustly in prison) and are about to embark on new villainy, there comes to Mynde "from farre" the admonishing voice of Wisdom. Rapidly the action returns to the symbolic plane of the opening scene. Wisdom (who must enter soon even if his first speech is heard from offstage) is assuredly dressed in the emblematic, unrealistic garb of scene i. And the Mights are suddenly once again parts of Mankynde's soul, even though still dressed, with jarring inconsistency, as the individual proud gallants of the life in sin. "O thou Mynde, remembyr the!" cries Wisdom (l. 873). Recalling the universal truth of the theological plays that "Dethe to every creature certen ys," he identifies himself and pleads: "Se in what stat thou doyst indwell!" But truth is at first slow to penetrate, and Mankynde cannot without a more palpable demonstration see his state as it is. "To my mynde," Mankynde says, through the voice of his Mynde, "yt cummyth from farre, / That dowtles man xall dey. / Ande thes weys we goe, we erre" (ll. 881–83), but his Understanding and Wyll are as yet unreached by any sense of error. So Wisdom produces the soul that they have unwittingly corrupted. "Here," according to the stage direction, "ANIMA apperythe in the most horrybull wyse, fowlere than a fende." And as Anima appears before Mankynde, Wisdom urges him "Se howe ye have dysvyguryde yowr soule! / Beholde yowrselff; loke veryly in mynde!" (ll. 901–2). As the Mights, parts of the soul, stare at the foul image of Anima, Mankynde is indeed beholding himself. The dramatist has externalized on stage Mankynde's inner realization of his transformation of what was, as Wisdom comments (ll. 905–8), God's own glorious place into a retreat of the Devil. So to "defoule" the soul was "onkynde," alien to man's proper nature.

The dramatist's instinct to depict vividly the soul's corruption as a stage spectacle carries him yet farther. Lucifer himself, regrettably, is not present, probably for the practical reason that with five speaking characters on stage no one is available to play him. In his stead is a set of minor devils, hidden as yet out of sight and literally occupying the soul. Wisdom goes on to say (ll. 909–12) that for the deadly sins Mankynde has used "So many devllys in yowr soule be. . . . Alas, man, of thi Soule have pyte!" According to a second quaint direction, there now "rennyt owt from wndyr the horrybyll mantyll of the SOULL seven small boys in the lykness of dewyllys and so retorne ageyn." We learn a few lines later in the text (l. 979) that they are "devllys blake," and quite possibly the mantle is the same, black and "fowle," that Anima had worn over her beautiful white gown in scene i. The boy-devils, as Bevington remarks, are no doubt the same mutes who supplied the Wits in the opening scene and danced as maintainers, perjurers, and "harlottys" in the ballets of sin. The frightening spectacle to which they contribute brings all three parts of the soul, not only Mynde, in Anima's words (l. 953) "to have knowynge they ill wrought." Understanding fears "Endles peyn worthyi be owr dysyrvynge," and Wyll desires to return to God and a new beginning.

Characteristically, the playwright has refashioned almost as a scene of masque the older form of recognition known to us from the ending (ll. 1263ff.) of the first temptation play in the *Castell* MS. There, it will be recalled, in a scene that does not correspond to anything in Macbeth's experience, the Good Angel, forsaken like Wisdom and mourning as the Prologue puts it "that the lofly lyknesse of God schulde be lore, / thorwe the badde aungellis fals entysynge," sends to Mankynde as he sits amidst the Deadly Sins the Christian admonition of Schrift: "behold thynne hert, . . . thynne owyn consyense." Penitencia, reaching with his lance to the heart of Mankynde, tells him that God asks no more "but sorwe of hert, with wepynge eye," and Mankynde cries "owte on the, dedly synne" and proceeds through "the sacrament / Of penauns" before entering the castle. Malus Angelus will have a second chance, however. In *Wisdom* for the first time (and again in *Mankind*) realization and contrition precipitated by the voice of moral truth end Mankynde's experience by motivating the resolution of the play as a whole.

This illuminating confrontation with self in *Wisdom* is the prototype of several recognition scenes occurring at the same point in post-theological Tudor dramas of temptation. It anticipates most strikingly the moment imagined by John Redford in which Wyt, disfigured in his sleep to resemble Ignorance, peers at himself in his glass of Reason and exclaims in amazement, "Gogs sowle a foole / a foole by the mas!" In *Othello* it enters for the first time into the realm of secular tragedy, and as it does so reminiscences of the technique and the love-theology of *Wisdom* flood back to it. Othello's perception that he is "Foole, foole, foole!" occurs in a scene to which an abundance of terms like "Soule," "Heaven," "Grace," "Angell," and "Divel" along with corresponding images have given strong religious overtones. More centrally, his discovery and acknowledgment of his terrible error leads to a process of tragic regeneration of spirit which, like the comic regeneration of Wyt, runs parallel to the religious regeneration of Mankynde though without any bearing on the afterlife. As a rule, the Tudor successor of Christ-Wisdom in his function as Christian admonisher is a personified abstraction like Reason, Verity, or Knowledge of Sinne. Shakespeare invests the role in the quite nonallegorical personage of Emilia.

Emilia turns Othello back from jealousy to the condition of love for Desdemona in which he began the play and in which he dies. Until she chides him, Othello remains in the disordered condition of spirit which Iago had brought about by deluding his reason so that the irrational forces of passion might take over. As noted, it is significant that he stepped into the chamber from the scene of riot, violence, and bloodshed in which Iago destroyed Roderigo and sought to kill Cassio. Now, even though he can speak musical lines about the unnamed "Cause" for which he supposes he must kill Desdemona, Othello is still disfigured from his true, noble nature. Shakespeare includes these lines to emphasize the irony and irrevocability of what Othello is about to do. His true condition (and the manner in which the actor is to play him) is specified in Desdemona's description of him. His eyes "rowle" and he gnaws his nether lip. "Some bloody passion," she adds, "shakes your very Frame" (ll. 38, 43–44). These words, reminiscent of Lodovico's exclamation in the scene (IV, i) wherein Othello struck her and departed murmuring of goats and monkeys, show that he is not himself and that the deed he is about to do is a murder, not a sacrifice, the expression in action of a state of spirit that has existed ever since the temptation scene.

Emilia reestablishes Othello's reason by exposing the villainy of her husband through her knowledge of the real history of the handkerchief, not primarily by exhibiting Othello's true state to him as in *Wisdom*. Yet she does paint him in the likeness of a fiend, calling him "the blacker Divell," and crying again "thou art a divell," as soon as she grasps what he has done. (The stage effect of these words would be immensely enhanced were Othello here dressed in black, and possibly Emilia's words are among the many implicit stage directions in the dialogue of *Othello*. They would sound strange addressed to an Othello gowned all in white.) When she perceives through his reference to her husband that "Villany hath made mockes with love" she calls Othello "Gull" and "dolt, / As ignorant as durt." Though "Heaven, and Men, and Divels" all cry shame against her, she will speak the truth about her husband—who then stabs her and flees, confirming that truth. "She lov'd thee, cruell Moore," she says finally, "So come my Soule to blisse, as I speake true."

Emilia's comparison of Othello to a black devil, and perhaps also her additional charges that Desdemona made a "filthy Bargaine" in marrying him and that he is now as ignorant as dirt, recall the projected image of the soul "fowlere than a fende," as the epithets "Gull," "dolt," and "Foole" echo Tudor scenes of recognition. And as in *Wisdom*, the hero's discovery that he has wrought ill raises the possibility of damnation. Mankynde's Understanding, we have noted, finds endless pain to be "owr dysyryvynge," and Wisdom at several points stresses the idea that those who "endyn yll, they goo to hell" (1. 878). Othello raises the possibility early in Emilia's tirade:

> O, I were damn'd beneath all depth in hell:
> But that I did proceed upon just grounds
> To this extremity.   (V, ii, 137–39)

Emilia removes any just grounds and proves the truth of her own comment: "This deede of thine is no more worthy Heaven / Then thou was't worthy her" (V, ii, 160–61).

In both plays the idea of Hell is curiously interwoven with the idea of love. It is just as the black devils dart out from the mantle of the Soul that Wisdom speaks most nearly in the accents of Desdemona:

> What have I do? why lowyste thou not me?
> Why cherysyste thi enmye? why hatyst thou thi frende?
> Myght I have don ony more for the?
> (ll. 913–15)

So Desdemona says her only sins are "Loves I beare you" and protests, "I never did / Offend you in my life" (ll. 40, 58–59). Wisdom, because he is Christ, judge and agent of creation as well as spouse of Mankynde, can modulate from pathetic to fearsome:

But love may brynge drede to mynde.

Thou hast made the a bronde of hell
Whom I made the ymage of lyght. . . .

(ll. 916–18)

Desdemona of course has only the one capacity; she cannot threaten damnation. But after Iago has killed Emilia and fled the scene, confirming like the black devils in *Wisdom* the hero's vision of his folly, and after Othello has rejected his own momentary base impulse to escape, he sees and touches Desdemona, and renewed love brings with it dread:

> Now: how dost thou looke now? Oh ill-Starr'd wench,
> Pale as thy Smocke: when we shall meete at compt,
> This looke of thine will hurle my Soule from Heaven,
> And Fiends will snatch at it. Cold, cold, my Girle?
> Even like thy Chastity. O cursed, cursed Slave!
> Whip me ye Divels,
> From the possession of this Heavenly sight:
> Blow me about in windes, roast me in Sulphure,
> Wash me in steepe-downe gulfes of Liquid fire.
> Oh *Desdemon!* dead *Desdemon!*: dead. Oh, oh!
>
> (V, ii, 272–81)

For the last time Desdemona is associated with Heaven and infidelity to her with damnation of the soul. At this point Iago is again brought forth.

The moral recognition of Mankynde's Mynde, Understanding, and Wyll in *Wisdom* would be yet sharper than it is, and the earlier commitments of the playwright more fully carried through, if Lucifer were returned and unmasked or at least if Wisdom were explicitly to say that the goodly gallant who had talked so glibly with them had been in fact the Devil. The deception in the temptation scene needs to be dispelled in the recognition scene, but it is dispelled only by implication. The nearest approach of Christ-Wisdom to explicitness in this matter is in the following passage, spoken just after the lines about the brand of Hell:

Yff the Devll myght, he wolde the qwell,
   But that mercy expellyt hys myght.
   Wy doyst thou, Soule, me all dyspyght?
      Why yewyst [givest] thou myn enmy that I have wrought?
   Why werkyst thou hys consell? by myn settys lyght?
   Why hatyst thou vertu? Why lovyst that ys nought?
                              (ll. 919–24)

It is only vaguely implicit that the glib gallant was "the Devll" and
that sin and the danger of damnation were results of "*hys* consell."
In the stanza of recognition which each of the three warders of the
soul now speaks there is awareness that they have sinned and have
defiled it, but nothing to release the pent-up knowledge in the
audience that the friendly young man of scene iii was really the soul's
great enemy. It may be the playwright's preoccupation with the
stage-picture of the corrupted soul or with exposition of the theology
of salvation that keeps him from exploiting here the dramatic
possibility latent in his use of the goodly gallant.

Shakespeare has the advantage of being able to have the tempter
present, and he makes full use of Othello's rejection of the false
image of Iago as an "honest man" who "hates the slime / That
stickes on filthy deeds" (V, ii, 148–49) and as his "Friend," Emilia's
husband, "honest, honest *Iago.*" What Othello comes finally to
perceive Iago to be matches what Mankynde would have realized had
the medieval dramatist exploited the relationship between his scenes
of temptation and recognition, not precisely that Iago is the Devil
in the guise of a twenty-eight-year-old honest man, but that he is a
"demy-Divell" who has, like the Devil, ensnared Othello's soul and
body. The term means, I have argued, that the character represents
a human being in Lucifer's role. Now he can be caught and will be
tortured. When Othello pricks him, does he not bleed? He is, as
the Dramatis Personae in the Folio says, "a Villaine," and according
to Lodovico "hath part confest his Villany." But unlike other villains
he has, in addition to much other harm, corrupted the very soul of the
protagonist.

In both dramas, recognition of folly leads to contrition and spiritual restoration as love flows back into the hero's relationship with his love-object; the sharp differences are those between the religious, allegorical mode and its tragic equivalent. After the three Mights have expressed realization of the error of their ways, Anima asks why is it that she, the soul, changes not but still lies "horryble in synne" even though "Mynde, Wyll, and Wndyrstondynge be brought / To have knowynge they ill wrought" (ll. 952–53). Wisdom answers that "very contrycyon" is also necessary, "A tere of the ey, with sorow veray, / That rubbyt and waschyt the Soule wythin" (ll. 963–64). Sorrow of heart

> . . . in especyall reformyth man,
> Ande makyt hym as clene as when he begane.
> Go seke this medsyne, Soull! (ll. 968–70)

Contrition is to be had through the Understanding. Mankynde will make confession, as he had achieved recognition, with the Mynde, and through the Wyll complete his part of the sacrament, "du satysfaccion." As Anima begins to weep, the devils under her mantle allegorically recede from the stage, even though the soul is still in deadly sin. The parts of the soul leave in procession for Holy Church, singing, the stage direction specifies, "as yt ys songyn in the passyon wyke," these verses from the Lamentations of Jeremiah: "Magna velud mare contricio, contricio tua: quis consoletur tui?" (2.13) and "Plorans ploravit in nocte, et lacrime eius in maxillis eius" (1.2). While the parts of the soul are offstage getting their costumes changed back to white, Wisdom beguiles the time somewhat awkwardly by reciting for the audience the nine points pleasing to God.

Once his recognition of his tragic folly has been doubly confirmed by the letters from Roderigo's pocket, Othello likewise weeps the tears of contrition. He asks that the Venetian officers report him as among other things one

> whose subdu'd Eyes,
> Albeit un-used to the melting moode,

> Drops teares as fast as the Arabian Trees
> Their Medicinable gumme. (V, ii, 348–51)

Like so many other passages in the play these lines contain an implicit direction to the actor, in this case that he must weep, and
thus in the theater carry more than the force of words only. Whether
or not we think that a tragic hero should weep at the last, Othello
does. And if the "Medicinable" quality in his simile associates itself
with his tears as well as with the gum of Arabian trees, as it would
seem to, then their equivalence is all the more clear to the "medsyne"
that purges and restores the soul of Mankynde. With his last breath
Othello reembraces the wife and mainstay of his better nature as
Mankynde will presently do, and dies upon a kiss.

Here contrition and restoration are wholly translated to actual
terms appropriate to tragedy. Othello's tears are part of the process
by which he becomes once again the noble Moor of Acts I and II
whom passion could not shake and who loved Desdemona. After
his fluctuations of behavior during his awakening to the truth, in
his penultimate speech he resumes the eloquence bespeaking inner
order that he had exhibited in defending his marriage before the
Duke. By recalling in connection with suicide his decisive treatment
in Aleppo once of a malignant Turk who traduced the state, Othello
has in a sense resumed his "occupation." Manifestly from his last
speech and the tragic loading of the bed, he is also restored to the
place where, as he once put it,

> I have garnerd up my heart,
> Where either I must live, or beare no life,
> The Fountaine from the which my currant runnes,
> Or else dries up.   (IV, ii, 57–60)

The "hellish villaine" remains on stage, but Othello is free of him.
There is however no hint that he is restored to grace in the technical,
religious sense. He is restored to the secular equivalent of grace as
defined at the outset of the action. Neither I think do the overtones
of spiritual damnation earlier in the scene mean that his soul is

damned. Othello said that he merited Hell, to be sure. He said so because he stands for an actual man who would speak in these terms under the circumstances. We may argue the "damnation" or "salvation" of Othello only if we apply analogically to Othello's actual life these terms which apply literally in the symbolic last scene of *Wisdom*, if we use them, that is, in a spiritual and moral sense that divorces them from Christian eschatology.[8]

This is to say again that Desdemona is not a Christ-figure but the spiritual equivalent in Othello's concrete and particular experience of Christ-Wisdom in Mankynde's symbolic and generalized experience. One may ingeniously cite evidence seeming to identify her with Christ, such as Othello's ironic and prophetic comment while she sleeps, "Be thus when thou art dead, and I will kill thee, / And love thee after," or his implicit identification of himself (in the Folio text) with the base Judean who caused the death of Christ, or even her dying effort to save him from punishment from her death. But she is not at all to be the agent of Othello's coming to bliss in Heaven. Indeed, so far as his agonized imaginings go, her aspect there will hurl his soul into Hell, where fiends will snatch at it. Christ-Wisdom has not been slandered as she has—however much more coherent and powerful the drama might have been in that event— and she ends less closely related to the metaphorical spouse of each chosen soul than Iago is to Lucifer, perhaps in part because her role has gone through a series of more realistic and human reenactments than has Iago's. Desdemona is a finer Grissell, the object of a contemplation and love which give order and meaning to the experience of Othello as the play depicts it, and while he loves her not, all is folly, passion, and disorder.

Man's reentrance at line 1064 of *Wisdom* restores the tableau with which the play opened. The stage direction specifies that the five Wits (acted no doubt by five of the mutes who were the black devils) shall precede Anima, with Mynde on one side of her and Understanding on the other, and Wyll following. All are dressed in their "fyrst clothynge" with their "chapplettys and crestys." All now wear "crownys," a detail not specified in the directions for scene i, although Wisdom there remarked that the clean soul stands as a king and that by resisting evil "xall have the crown of glory, / That ys everlastynge joy" (ll. 307–8). It is not specified whether Anima still wears the mantle of black symbolic of Mankynde's sensuality. Presumably not.

The action of *Wisdom* is now virtually over, and the remaining hundred lines are devoted to comment by Anima, Wisdom, and the three Mights upon the soul's reformation. Anima, though given grace by Holy Church, knows that she may not alone "satysfye my trespas" and turns for aid to Christ-Wisdom, who is now all mercy:

> By the recognycion ye have clere,
> Ande by the hye lowe ye have godly,
> It perrysschyt my hert to here yow crye,
> Now ye have forsake synne and be contryte,
> Ye were never so leve to me verelye.
> Now ye be reformyde to yowr bewtys bryght.
>
> (ll. 1087–92)

Wisdom has already made on the cross the unique satisfaction that man alone is "impotent" to make, and by the sacrament of penance the soul has now been cleansed of actual sin as it had been by the sacrament of baptism of original sin. Never again, now crowned as he is to reign in endless bliss, should Mankynde disfigure himself to the likeness of the Fiend.

Both the recognition that Mankynde has had and the high love he has regained are wholly salvific. They restore the soul's eligibility for Heaven. *Othello*, as we have seen in Chapter II, is not the first secular play to adapt realization and penance as dramatic forms less relevant to Heaven, though its concomitant stress upon a bond of love is unexampled in the last scenes of the Tudor interludes in question. But *Othello* is the first and only English temptation play to fuse the restorative recognition and contrition with unrelieved tragedy. *Macbeth*, written as we think some two years later, is another tragedy of temptation and tragic realization, but realization for Macbeth leads to desolation, not to contrition, not to tears. Like the bleak death of Mankynde in *The Castell of Perseverance*, it has nothing to do with the sacrament of penance. Here a process akin to that sacrament restores Othello so that he may die as the noble spirit married to Desdemona whom we met at the outset. The effect of his being thus restored is to heighten and intensify our sense of tragic loss at his death, not to diminish or annul it.

The rapid catastrophe of *Othello* leaves no room for the leisured comment that accompanies the reformation of Mankynde in *Wisdom* to his beauties bright. Shakespeare cannot take the action back to the secure world of Venice where it began, though his introduction of Lodovico, Gratiano, and other officers together with Othello's unvarnished account of himself to them and several references to the Venetian state in the last forty lines of the play does recall Act I and the more elaborate portrait there of Othello with his perfect soul. There is no way to tell whether Shakespeare meant to express the reformation of the Moor by investing him all in white as with Mankynde; Othello might put on a white cape or gown when Lodovico says, "Come, bring away" (1. 337). Nonetheless Othello after his clear recognition of his folly enacts something notably similar to the sacrament that underlies the conclusion of *Wisdom*. He makes confession: that he loved not wisely, but too well, and, being wrought, was perplexed in the extreme; that he threw a pearl away. His subdued eyes drop upon his cheeks tears of contrition. He makes satisfaction appropriate to his nature and to the tragic theater.

CHAPTER V

The King of Life in King Lear

> They flatter'd me like a Dogge, and told mee I had the white
> hayres in my Beard, ere the blacke ones were there. To say I, and
> no, to every thing that I said: I, and no too, was no good
> Divinity. . . . Go too, they are not men o' their words; they told
> me, I was every thing: 'Tis a Lye, I am not Agu proofe.
> —*King Lear*

The oldest of the English moral dramas survives in a difficult and
fragmentary manuscript from the Account Roll of the Priory of the
Holy Trinity, Dublin. It represented for the medieval audience
gathered round it the proud folly of the King of Life, his agon
with Death, his salvation through the intercession of Our Lady. That
audience seems to have been as universal as the meaning of the
action which it viewed—

> ric & por, yong & hold,
> men & wemen that bet her,
> bot lerit & leut, stout & bold!
>
> Lordinge & ladiis that beth hende. . . .
>
> (ll. 2–5)

The staging was evidently the medieval theater in the round employed
for the more fully developed moral play *The Castell of Perseverance*
(ca. 1405) and for the Cornish mystery plays: in this theater scaffolds
in which actors might recite their lines or from which they might
descend to do so were arranged about a broad, circular outdoor
placea or "place."[1] There is a prayer for good weather (l. 10), and
a reference to the pla[cea] occurs after line 470; the Bishop is found
sitting on his "se" (l. 323), and the King retires behind his
scaffold-curtains (l. 303). On the basis of less certain evidence,
partly philological, the play is thought to have been composed in the
south of England toward the end of the fourteenth century and to

have been brought to the north before being copied ca. 1400 in blank spaces of the Account Roll. It was discovered by James Mills of the Dublin Record Office, who printed it in 1891 and titled it *The Pride of Life*; it has been twice reedited.[2]

This play about the King of Life represents a truly new departure in English drama. Coming toward the close of the formative period of the great English cycles that staged the history of the race from Creation to Judgment, *The Pride of Life* breaks quite free from biblical history. While it may possibly have been inspired by a southern English play on the death of King Herod, it escapes under the light touch of allegory into a realm where the playwright can shape events independently and turn his primary attention away from the history of the race to the typical experience of the human individual. He chooses to focus upon the individual's encounter with death and to represent him by a king. Despite the happy ending in Heaven which he appends, in so choosing he fashions his new kind of drama as tragedy, and he writes with a sure hand. C. M. Gayley justly praises *The Pride of Life* "not so much for its lofty and ideal conception as for the excellence with which it portrays ingenuous and fundamental types of character, and conducts a plot straightforward, tragic and severe, the natural outgrowth of premises common to the play and to a contemporary view of life."[3]

My present purpose is to compare *The Pride of Life* with *King Lear* and demonstrate what seems to me the striking kinship between the King of Life and Shakespeare's King Lear in the pattern and significance of their tragic experience. This is, I think, part of Shakespeare's return to the structure of moral drama in his three great early Jacobean tragedies, *Othello* and *Macbeth* being related to the morality plays of temptation as *King Lear* is to those on the coming of death. Again, the historical relationship has interpretive value. From the point of view of *The Pride of Life* we may regard *King Lear* with fresh eyes, our critical faculties alerted and guided in a new way.

In this view, for example, the ceremonial opening scene of the tragedy takes on new overtones that we find to be reinforced later in the play, and we may begin to understand why Shakespeare had

Edgar assume the disguise of Poor Tom rather than some other disguise, and why he had the Foul Fiend haunt him. At a level of universal relevance, the experience of each protagonist, kingly exemplar of human vanity, is the same: first, his initial pride and violent wrath, with trust in flattery and scorn for truth, especially when it is uttered by the woman who loves him in her heart; second, the chastening agony of the middle phase of the action, with its illuminating failure of those upon whom he had depended and his recognition of spiritual truths; third, his restoration through the kindness of "a Soule in blisse." Our first English play that is not, like a mystery play, an elaboration upon some earlier form of the same play and that does not recount a phase of biblical history or the life of a saint, thus conforms in broad outline to what is commonly regarded as the grandest expression of the English tragic spirit. The resemblance, as I hope to show, extends further, especially in the second phase of the plot, the agon, where several issues central and primary in the medieval play recur in Shakespeare.

If this resemblance, which seems (to me at least) so obvious when the plays are juxtaposed, has gone quite unnoticed hitherto, the reasons are not far to seek. Foremost is the general problem faced in this book, that traditional ideas about "influence" and "source" do not supply a calculus and vocabulary of literary relationships subtle enough to be of service in comparing works so different in mode after intuition has suggested that the comparison might be fruitful. Here it involves dramas separated by two hundred years in time of composition and corresponding distances in dramatic conventions and in genius, even though the ancient play with its religious figures, its type characters from courtly life, its personified abstraction Death, its allegory and alliterative quatrains, perhaps made within its round of fourteenth-century earth an equivalent dramatic impression to that of its counterpart at the Globe. But its crabbed, imperfect MS marks *The Pride of Life* as particularly remote and obscure, a curiosity for antiquarians. The MS, moreover, is fragmentary, breaking off after the first of the three main phases of the plot has been completed, the delineation of the King's initial rashness. The remainder is recounted in the Prologue and may fairly well be reconstructed by reference to kindred literature of the period, but the text has not lent itself to the anthologizing which makes a medieval play familiar to Shakespeare's critics. To some of these my resurrecting of *The Pride of Life* and juxtaposing it to *King Lear* at one stroke will appear to be as rash an act as Lear's division of his kingdom, and to warrant as violent a reaction.

Even the studies devoted to the medieval bearings of Renaissance English drama have slighted *The Pride of Life*, primarily, I should say, because the preconceptions of the evolutionist do not prepare him to discover intimate correspondence between the primitive and the last, most highly elaborated exemplars of a form, correspondence closer in fundamental respects than to any intermediates. At any rate, it seems simply not to have occurred to the scholars responsible for the large bibliography in this field to consider whether a great tragedy might sometimes be in important structural respects a throw-back to the theological prototypes of Tudor secular drama, though it is manifest that theology and tragedy have much in common. *The Pride of Life* falls into a special obscurity in this regard because it was not the idea of the play on the coming of death, but that of the temptation play, which Tudor dramatists adapted from Lancastrian drama, secularized, and elaborated upon. *The Pride of Life* and *Everyman* alone focus exclusively upon death's coming to the universally representative central figure of moral drama. A section of *The Castell of Perseverance*, the morality nearest in antiquity to *The Pride of Life*, likewise dramatizes the event, which does not occur again in the extant pre-Elizabethan drama. Because their point of attack lies late in the hero's life, the plays devoted to the coming of death lack the colorful tempters found in the temptation plays of the Macro MSS and subsequently in the secular moralities. Instead they feature wicked characters whose function is not to tempt but simply, and instructively, to fail, like Goneril and Regan, in time of need. Goneril and Regan are to Strength and Health, Fellowship, Cousin, and Goods, as Iago is to the Devil and the Vice. Everyman and the King of Life alone are already confirmed in vanity at the outset of the play, which is primarily about their bitter, salutary recognition of that vanity for what it is and subsequent painful adoption of a better set of values. The design, tied inseparably to eschatology, was of no use to the worldly didacticism of Tudor playwrights. For the modern student, of course, *The Pride of Life* lies along with the Macro plays in the shadow of the celebrated *Everyman*, whose fame is due not solely to its undoubted merit but to the accidents that preserved its text complete and in Tudor print. When in 1744 Robert Dodsley praised the moral dramas over the mysteries because the latter only followed "some miraculous History from the Old or New Testament" whereas "in these *Moralities* something of design appeared, a Fable and a Moral,"[4] he had read none but *Everyman.* Bishop Percy, Warton, and Malone merely echo his words, and even today *Everyman* is often treated as if it were entirely representative. Though accessible, *Everyman* is not typical, probably not indigenous to England. The student in the standard course who reads it and turns to Marlowe is poorly equipped to discover what has happened to the allegorical drama in *Doctor Faustus.* In my judgment he is better prepared to study the medieval bearings of *King Lear,* even though *Lear* lacks the obvious fossils of archaic technique preserved in *Faustus.*

Yet the sole published study that supplies precedent for the present approach to *King Lear* takes over the traditional assumption that *Everyman* may stand for all moral drama. Oscar Campbell in "The Salvation of Lear" calls Shakespeare's tragedy a "sublime morality play" and emphasizes the homiletic stories of false friendship that lie behind and influence *Everyman.*[5] He does not observe that the tradition of fifteenth- and sixteenth-century moral drama is of plays of temptation primarily rather than of exposure of false friends at death. Though preoccupied with the coming of death, he does not mention *The Pride of Life.* But indubitably that older and more certainly indigenous drama is the more closely paralleled in *King Lear.* Its hero is a proud king who falls to death through an incredible, tragic error in judgment, this error perpetrated in the opening scene. Everyman, in contrast, is a gay and wealthy dandy, not a king, and he is by far a meeker and more passive figure than either Lear or the King of Life. The King of Life, moreover, is a king of Britain as well, and in this capacity he bestows, as reward for flattery, the

castle of Gailispire in Berkshire and, creating an uncanny if fortuitous
link with Shakespeare's play, the earldom of Kent. There are other
such links, perhaps the most interesting being that according to
Brandl the boy Solas who sits on the King's knee may be related to
the court fool.[6] On the whole, *The Pride of Life* resembles *King Lear*
in its structure more than does *Everyman*, despite the parallel which
Campbell stresses between Everyman's pilgrimage from one vain
attachment to another and Lear's traveling to Goneril and Regan.
Unlike the opening of *Everyman*, in which God sends Death to tell
the protagonist that his time is up, that of *The Pride of Life* is
genuinely equivalent to Shakespeare's. The moribund King at once
reveals his character and rash determination to commit an act of
desperate folly, his perverse inability to recognize flattery for what
it is and to accept good counsel. Everyman, surprised by God's
messenger Death, reveals only his naiveté and starts a relatively
quiet journey in quest of the real values in life. The group of
characters on stage at the outset of *The Pride of Life* resembles
what we find in Shakespeare's opening scene, the dominant, irascible
protagonist together with several comparatively flat and predictable
characters standing either for truth or vanity. The King is individualized by his hair-trigger wrath and masculine contempt for women's
words as well as generalized by his role and name to represent the
principle of proud life. Indeed, up until the entrance of Death midway in *The Pride of Life* this older play seems far less thoroughly
infiltrated by theology and altogether more concrete and realistic
than *Everyman*, and to an extent this may have been true in the latter
half of the play as well. Queen, Bishop, even the flattering knights
and boy messenger are "ingenuous types," not really personifications.
For although the knights are nominally Strength and Health, they
talk like knights and do not assume full allegorical significance until
they fail to conquer Death. Solas, or Mirth, assumes little or no such
significance. Later in the play, Our Lady, the Soul, the fiends, Christ,
and God are spiritual but also concrete figures, not abstractions.
Only Death is a thoroughgoing personification of an abstraction.

The King, unlike Everyman except when Everyman scourges
himself, endures physical suffering and debasement, and in doing so

it is very likely that, with Lear, he comes to perceive his human kinship with the poor. Unlike Everyman's spiritual recognition, finally,
his is utterly tragic. For though it might perhaps have won the
sympathy of the audience, being recognition too late it could not
of itself permit him to gain salvation. It is not, like that of Everyman and like the recognition scenes in *Wisdom, Mankind,* and
many a Tudor moral interlude, didactic; it is hardly the author's
intent to preach that we should perceive the vanity of the world
only after death has already struck us down. Nor is the touching
dénouement didactic, as would have been the damnation of the
King's soul. Like what Campbell calls the salvation of Lear, the
salvation of the King of Life is accomplished by an act of gratuitous
compassion. "You do me wrong to take me out o'th'grave, / Thou art
a Soule in blisse. . . ." Lear's words spoken after the close of his own
agon (IV, vii, 45–46) might appropriately have been said, with strict
literalness, by the King of Life to Our Lady. In such a way, the
underlying meanings of the tragedy of Lear as his deranged mind
sees them with the insight born of madness often correspond to
explicit meanings of *The Pride of Life.* This is particularly true of
the theme of social criticism shared by the plays. It concerns itself
with the injustice suffered by the poor at the hands of the rich and is
intimately connected with their common moral: Take physic, Pomp.

Initial Folly

The Pride of Life, after its Prologue, opens on a haughty speech by
the King, in this vein:

> king ic am, kinde of kinges i korre,
> Al the worlde wide to welde at my wil;
> Nas ther never no man of woman i borre
> O gein me with stonde, that i nold him spille.
> (ll. 121–24)

Students of the English mystery plays will catch echoes of the voice
of Herod. Rex Vivus (as the speech headings name him) has about
him two knights or soldiers. Strength tells him that he need fear

nothing that may befall, and Health assures him that he will live forever. Further boasting on his part is interrupted by the Queen, a bearer of sermon influence into the play. His queen, who loves him in her heart, reminds him therefore that he is mortal, that he had a beginning and should think about making a good ending. To this wisdom, the King reacts with unreasonable violence, and he claims to doubt her love for him. Rex Vivus heeds not a whit her further reminder that Death overcomes all things and her advice that he serve God. "Qwhat say ye?" he asks the knights, Primus Miles Fortitudo and Secundus Miles Sanitas, the first of whom promises to withstand Death and make his sides bleed. And II Miles, sounding more like one of Herod's soldiers than like Health, adds that he would lance Death if he met him in field or street. The gratified protagonist summons Mirth and asks him whether any man whom the boy has met "dorst with me to strive." Mirth gives the desired reply and for this flattery receives a castle and becomes Earl of Kent. His insouciance and opportunism suggest that he may be related to the same class of extra-dramatic entertainers that later supplied the Vice.[7] If Solas is the fool, he is not altogether fool, but neither is he the needling voice of conscience that Lear's Fool is.

As Rex Vivus retires behind the curtain of his scaffold, the dramatist, consciously or not, manages a fine irony in the balance of mortal frailty against pride in strength:

> Draw the cord, sire streynth,
> Rest I wol now take;
> On erth in brede ne leynth
> Ne was nere yet my make.
>
> (ll. 303–6)

This, again, is an Herodian detail.[8]

His queen at once instructs the messenger to fetch the Bishop of the land, who she hopes can more successfully preach than she to this King who is "in siche errour broght." The Bishop preaches at greater length but not to more effect. Rex Vivus calls him "bissop-babler" and tells him to go home and learn to preach better. With rash effrontery, the King sends his messenger to seek out and challenge Death, and Mirth is on his way to do so as the extant part of the play breaks off.

These events of the surviving fragment of the play are summarized in the first eighty lines of the Prologue, the last thirty-two lines of which tell how the play ended. Death—the King of Death, Mirth calls him—comes, spreading universal destruction, and encounters the King of Life. He "dredit no thing his knightis" and "delith him depe dethis wounde." Sorrow awakes the soul. Fiends snatch it, and it has a dispute with the body. Our Lady "wol prey her son so mylde" that it be left in her keeping.

In the pattern of kingly folly and consequent suffering common to these plays, Act I, scene i, of *Lear* is equivalent to the extant part of *The Pride of Life*. It happens that the depiction of the initial vanity of Rex Vivus is divided in two so that Solas, the messenger, may fetch the Bishop on the Queen's behalf. The King of Life sleeps inside his scaffold while the Bishop speaks a long choral monologue on the state of the world of which Rex Vivus has boasted that he is king. His theme, the social vices owing to the unequal distribution of wealth, enters *King Lear* at a later point. But altogether the King of Life is before the audience during about 350 lines, of which he speaks over 140. These clearly constitute the whole initial phase of the action, for the Prologue explicitly places the start of the agon after the sending of the message to Death which closes the extant fragment. Lear is on stage for 231 lines during his first appearance and speaks 120, so that the two proud kings are introduced at comparable length. Lear's moral awakening likewise begins in the next scene (I, iv) in which he appears, although it begins more gradually than that of Rex Vivus must have done.

The material for Shakespeare's opening scene—the competition of three daughters in a show of love, the division of the kingdom, the suitors for Cordelia—comes, of course, from his sources. But much the same material went into the old play *Leir,* which bears no special resemblance in design to the plot of the coming of death. Shakespeare, unlike the author of *Leir,* characterizes the protagonist at the outset through his acts of proud folly and vanity and conceives the remainder of the main plot in terms of physical disaster and spiritual heightening, of tragic realization. There remains nothing allegorical about the plot. All is concrete and literal as in earlier versions of Lear's career. Lear does not take assurance from such general transitory things as strength and health; indeed he wants to confer all cares and business upon "yonger strengths" and thus "un-burthen'd crawle toward death" (I, i, 39–41). Rather he takes assurance from the still-soliciting eyes and the voices, reverberating hollowness, of daughters equally untrustworthy as are Strength and Health to mortal man. His personal and political folly has the same force as the theological folly of the King of Life. Lear keeps the pomp of kingship, "The name, and all th'addition to a King" (I, i, 136). But, like Gorboduc, he surrenders the substance of rule, part-ing Britain between his sons-in-law. Similarly he mistakes the out-ward show of love and loyalty in Goneril and Regan for the reality in Cordelia and Kent. Goneril and Regan are not abstractions, but nonetheless it is simply in their nature to be false as it is in the nature of Strength and Health and of Fellowship, Kindred, and Goods. The whole ceremony which Lear wants enacted is pompous and hollow.

Lear's touchiness bears comparison with that of Rex Vivus. Both kings interpret just criticism of their behavior as betrayal. Rex Vivus complacently hears Primus Miles tell him to live as he lists, for no one made of blood and bone is so dependable as his darling Strength, and the second knight guarantees him immortality. In the religious and allegorical context of *The Pride of Life*, this pair of testimonials feeds the vanity of Rex Vivus as the twin speeches of Goneril and Regan feed Lear's, by telling him what he wants to hear. But then, in each case, the proud monarch must listen to the low voice of truth from a woman. His lady, who the Prologue tells us "is lettrit in lor, / as cumli becomit for a quen" and "lovit him gostlic in hert," punctures the bubble of his vanity with truth and for thanks receives insult and recrimination:

> Sire, thou saist, as the liste;
> thou livist at thi wille.

bot somthing thou miste,
& ther ffor hold the stille:

thinke, thou haddist beginninge
Qwhen thou were i bore;
& bot thou mak god endinge,
thi sowle is fforlore.

love god & holy chirche
& have of him som eye;
ffonde his werkes for to wirch,
& thinke, that thou schal deye.

REX. douce dam, qwhi seistou so?
thou spekis noght as the sleye.
I schal lyve ever mo
ffor bothe two thin eye.

.woldistou that i were dede,
that thou might have a new?
hore, the devil gird of thi hede!
bot that worde schal the rewe!

(ll. 179–98)

Lear reacts with similar suspicion and wrath to the check placed upon his vanity by his loyal daughter. Each king interprets the woman's words to mean that she, who in fact loves him most, does not love him at all, and Lear, disclaiming at once for Cordelia all his "Paternall care, / Propinquity and property of blood," tries to make her rue the one word, "Nothing," which is her response to his request for flattery: "What can you say, to draw / A third, more opilent than your Sisters? speake." She cannot say, like Regan, that she is alone felicitate in his love, but young and true as she is, offers him the obedience, love, and honor fitting to a daughter. Lear, then, will give her no dower and holds her as a stranger to his heart. Again, the content of the scene is not explicitly the theology of the coming of death. In the pagan terms characteristic of the tragedy, Lear acknowledges the very mortality which Rex Vivus denies, for he can swear "By all the operation of the Orbes, / From whom we do exist and cease to be" (I, i, 111–12). Nonetheless, on its concrete or literal level Lear's perverse and violent reaction upon exposure to the hard truth is equivalent to that of Rex Vivus. Cordelia is denying filial affection no more than the wise Queen, in mentioning his mortality, means that she wishes the King of Life were dead. Cordelia stands in the same relation to Lear and his two false daughters as does the Queen to Rex Vivus and Strength and Health. Goneril and Regan, not being personified abstractions even in name, express a false love which has no allegorical significance. But their equivalence to Strength and Health, and to some of the flatterers of Everyman, is made vividly clear when the old king looks back upon this scene with the insight of his madness. In the rain and wind, and when the thunder would not peace at his bidding, there, like Rex Vivus in the stormy encounter with Death, he found them out. Their acquiescence to his whim was "no good Divinity." "Go too, they are not men o' their words; they told me, I was every thing: Tis a Lye, I am not Agu proofe" (IV, vi, 97ff.). The words are perfectly appropriate to the situation of the King of Life and his knights. It is later in the same scene that Lear wipes his hand because "It smelles of Mortality."

In both *The Pride of Life* and *King Lear*, there are two principal spokesmen for vanity and two for truth. Kent, like the Bishop, takes over from the good lady who has failed in her loving rebuke:

> what wouldest thou do old man?
> Think'st thou that dutie shall have dread to speake,
> When power to flattery bowes?
> To plainnesse honour's bound,
> When Majesty falls to folly, reserve thy state,
> And in thy best consideration checke
> This hideous rashnesse. . . .   (I, i, 148–53)

Even while Lear calls him "Vassall! Miscreant," Kent persists:

> . . . revoke thy guift,
> Or whil'st I can vent clamour from my throate,

Ile tell thee thou dost evill.   (I, i, 167–79)

Lear banishes Kent from the kingdom for his pains.

Episcopus, after his soliloquy on the state of the world, seeks ineffectively to caution its proud king. He repeats the lesson of the Queen and adds that Death is no man to spare Rex Vivus anything, that consequently the King should "do dedis of charite" and learn Christ's lore and live in Heaven's light to save his soul from sorrow. The response is at first sarcastic:

> wat, bissop, bissop-babler,
> schold y of det hav dred?
> thou art bot a chagler:
> go hom yi wey, i red!   (ll. 407–10)

In the next stanza Rex Vivus declares that, if the Bishop has come hither to affright him with Death, he wishes Bishop and Death were rotting in the sea together, and he soon works himself up into a fury:

> go hom, god yif ye sorow!
> thou wreist me in my mod.
> war woltou prec tomorou?
> thou nost uer, bi the rod!
>
> troust thou, I [u]old be ded
> In my [yi]ng lif?
> thou lisst, screu, bolhed:
> evil mot thou triwe!   (ll. 415–22)

Though he lives now as he lists, the Bishop concludes, Death will come right soon and wound him for his "outrage." Graved under the green, he shall take small consolation from his "gay croun of golde." Rex Vivus tells the departing Bishop to "lerne bet to preche." Thus, at the end of the demonstration of their pride, he and Lear alike have banished the voices of truth from their presence. Each now consummates the rashness which will plunge him into suffering and tragic realization. Rex Vivus, secure with his pitiful retinue ("my meyne" [l. 465]) of knights, sends off his challenge to Death.

And Lear, banishing Kent and denying Cordelia, commits his old age to the professed bosoms of Goneril and Regan—and as we soon discover to his own noisy and vain retinue of knights.

Agon and Recognition

In *The Pride of Life* and *King Lear*, but in no intervening English play except *Everyman*, the hero's initial vanity plunges him into an agony of realization. This is followed by the salvation or restoration for which it has prepared him in spirit.

Although it can be shown that Lear's suffering more deeply resembles that of Rex Vivus than that of Everyman, the two scenes in which the old king is successively disabused about Goneril and Regan as a chronological and geographical sequence find their nearer parallel probably in *Everyman*. Everyman, as he says, undertakes a pilgrimage, whereas most likely Rex Vivus' two false friends betrayed him together in the same place. Because the agon of Rex Vivus must be reconstructed before it can be compared to that of Lear, *Everyman* offers the more obvious and convenient basis for suggesting the resemblance of the middle scenes of the main plot of *King Lear* to the agon of the coming of death.

Everyman,[9] as we have seen, does not like *King Lear* and *The Pride of Life* open with a scene designed to demonstrate the protagonist's vain attachment to the false values in his life, but this attachment is implied by his response to the summons delivered by Death. Naively, he goes to Fellowship, to his Kindred and Cousin, and then to Goods. He is successively disappointed by each yet still expects the next worldly contact to sustain him, until he is finally and most bitterly disappointed by Goods. Only then, when he thinks that he is lost, does he stumble upon his hitherto unregarded Good Deeds, who alone can introduce him to the Knowledge that leads through the offices of Holy Church to salvation.

Everyman's friends represent increasingly close bonds with worldliness and so they are increasingly sarcastic and vicious in refusing to help him. Fellowship merely declares that if it were a question of food, drink, women, or murder, he would be glad to oblige, but under the circumstances he can only wish Everyman godspeed. Cousin transparently claims to have "the crampe in my to[e]," declaring in the same breath, "Trust not to me; . . . / I wyll deceyve you in your moost nede" (ll. 356–58). Kindred says facetiously that she will give her maid leave to help Everyman, if the two of them can agree. Goods, openly despiteful, arouses Everyman's first outburst of passion:

> O false Good! cursed thou be,
> Thou traytour to God, that hast deceyved me
> And caugh[t] me in thy snare! (ll. 451–53)

As Goods laughs, Everyman cries out in accents of Lear, "A, Good, thou hast had longe my hertely love, / I gave the[e] that which sholde be the Lorde's above . . ." (ll. 457–58). Alone, Everyman says that these encounters have made him ashamed, that he is worthy of blame and may well hate himself. Lear too by this point in the action, it will be recalled, feels a burning shame that detains him from Cordelia.

The first episode in Lear's similar disenchantment with his false daughters occurs in Act I, scene iv, of the tragedy. We have already heard Goneril, in the manner of Cousin, tell Oswald to "say I am sicke" (I, iii, 8) and to come slack of former services, and Lear himself has already perceived a faint neglect and purpose of un-kindness, as he puts it, in Albany's establishment. Now, as the Fool probes the folly of Lear's having given away all the titles but the one he was born with, Goneril asks him to reduce his precious retinue of knights and thus reveals herself as no daughter at all. By contrast he sees how small was the fault in Cordelia that drew all love from his heart. But he can still say "I have another daughter, / Who I am sure is kinde and comfortable" and mean Regan, and his old rash-ness and temper are undiminished. Outside (I, v), half listening to the boy's wise foolery, he ponders Cordelia and Goneril: "I did her wrong. . . . Monster Ingratitude!"

Lear's scene with Regan (II, iv) corresponds to Everyman's inter-view with Goods. Lear regards her as his last hope for comfort, and so clings until the last possible moment to his illusion that she will sustain him. Though he shows for the first time traces of an ability to forbear rather than fly off the handle when he is crossed (ll. 105–9), Lear's rising passion becomes finally more overwhelming than when he cursed Goneril. He rushes forth to be scourged and humbled by the elements, to gain self-knowledge and understanding of the world, and to rediscover and be saved by Cordelia.

Lear's initial reaction to the stocking of his messenger Kent and to Cornwall's and Regan's denial of his request to speak at once with them is one of simple incredulity; it cannot be that they would behave thus toward him. When Regan appears he is still full of trust:

> Beloved *Regan*,
> Thy Sisters naught: oh *Regan*, she hath tied
> Sharpe-tooth'd unkindnesse, like a vulture heere,
> I can scarce speake to thee, thou'lt not beleeve
> With how deprav'd a quality. Oh *Regan*.
>   (II, iv, 135–39)

Her cold suggestion that he return to Goneril does not touch his faith, whose expression takes on increasing dramatic irony:

> No *Regan*, thou shalt never have my curse:
> Thy tender-hefted Nature shall not give
> Thee o're to harshnesse; Her eyes are fierce, but thine
> Do comfort, and not burne.   (II, iv, 173–76)

Not even when Goneril enters and Regan takes her by the hand can Lear end this wishful thinking. "Mend when thou can'st," he tells Goneril,

> be better at thy leisure,
> I can be patient, I can stay with *Regan*,
> I and my hundred Knights. (II, iv, 232–34)

When in response Regan says that she will give place to no more than twenty-five, Lear's reply (l. 252) echoes Everyman's protest to Goods: "I gave you all." It is only when, with loveless rationality, Regan asks, "What need one?" that the old man perceives the wretchedness of his plight and rushes from his comfortless daughters. The scene elaborates the simple scenes of disenchantment in *Everyman*, and the daughters are the descendants in concrete drama of such personified abstractions of false values as Kindred and Goods, akin to these prototypes as Iago is to the tempters in the temptation plays.

The middle portion of *The Pride of Life*, as well as the dénouement, is unfortunately lost. But it may be reconstituted, with at least a modicum of assurance, in what has been aptly called the flickering light of the Prologue. I shall have to attempt this reconstruction before comparing Lear's agon with that which the Prologue describes for Rex Vivus. The King's fight with Death, in which his two flattering knights of course fail him, and the dispute between his body and soul have their analogues in literature contemporary with and closely related to *The Pride of Life*. So does his salvation through the intercession of Our Lady. In actual drama, the experience of Everyman at the moment of his death, and particularly that of Mankynde in *The Castell of Perseverance*, can be shown on reasonably strong grounds to match the corresponding experience of the King of Life in important respects and hence to help us to visualize it. In dealing with certain other analogues, especially with the Dance of Death, we are perhaps also dealing with sources of *The Pride of Life* and therefore with the very origins of English moral drama. But what matters here is that these analogues must bear an essential resemblance to the lost sections of *The Pride of Life* and other such plays which presumably existed but are not preserved in writing. It would be remarkable indeed if the play were unique, if the only such play which had existed in medieval England were preserved in the Dublin MS. Although the analogues suggested by its Prologue may not allow a reliable reconstruction of *The Pride of Life* in any detail, they doubtless suggest the kind of detail to be found in other dramatizations of the death of exemplars of human vanity like Rex Vivus.

The physical encounter in which Rex Vivus first had occasion to perceive the folly of his rashness and pride is described in the Prologue as follows:

> sone affter hit be fel, that deth & life,
> beth to geder i take

> & ginneth & strivith a sterne strife,
> king of life to wrake.
>
> with him drivith a doun to grounde,
> he dredit no thing his knightis
> & delith him depe dethis wounde
> & kith on him his mightis.   (ll. 85–92)

The Prologue then continues and, but for a quatrain asking the audience not to create disturbance, concludes with an account of the spiritual history of the King after death and of Our Lady's intercession in his behalf. In this portion of his Prologue, it seems likely that the author does not closely follow the order of events in the play itself:

> Qwhen the body is doun i broght
> the soule sorow a wakith;
> the bodyis pride is dere a boght:
> the soule the ffendis takith.
>
> & throgh priere of oure lady mylde
> al godenisse scho wol qwyte:
> scho wol prey her son so mylde,
> the soule & body schul dispyte.
>
> the cors that nere knewe of care,
> No more then stone in weye,
> schal . . . of sorow & sore care
> . . . be twene ham tweye.
>
> the soule ther on schal be weye,
> that the ffendes have i kaghte;
> & oure lady schal ther for preye,
> so that with her he schal be lafte.
>
> (ll. 93–108)

Judging from the analogues, the probable sequence of events was this: the fight with Death and the failure or desertion of Strength and Health, the dispute between the Body and Soul terminated by the coming of the fiends, the prayer of Our Lady to her Son, resulting in the rescue of Rex Vivus from danger of Hell. Perhaps she made her appearance earlier, however, or appeared twice, as the Prologue implies.

One of the unreliable minions of Rex Vivus, Strength, has his exact counterpart in *Everyman*. Without espousing Henry de Vocht's theory that *The Pride of Life* is a source of *Everyman*,[10] we may safely suppose a certain degree of resemblance between the roles of Strength in the two plays, especially when Strength addresses Everyman in the same tones of false comfort which his namesake addresses to Rex Vivus: "And I Strength wyll by you stande in dystres / Thou thou wolde in batayle fyght on the ground" (ll. 684–85). The fundamental difference in structure between these two English plays devoted wholly to the coming of death is that *Everyman* begins with the summons and ends with the quiet descent into the grave, whereas the action of *The Pride of Life* moves through the stormy encounter itself and into the afterlife. Hence in *Everyman* Strength is not asked to do actual battle. Nonetheless, along with Beauty, Discretion, and Five-Wits, he manages to fail the protagonist at the edge of the grave, in the equivalent moment to Rex Vivus' clash with Death.

> STRENGTH. I repent me that I [h]yder came.
> EVERYMAN. Strength you to dysplease I am to blame.
>   Wyll ye breke promyse that is dette?

Strength, be it noted, not only fails Everyman but turns against him:

> STRENGTH. In fayth, I care not.
>   Thou arte but a foole to complayne.
>   You spende your speche and wast your brayne.
>   Go thryst the[e] in to the grounde.

Everyman gives explicit voice to the bitter recognition which this reversal forces upon him:

> EVERYMAN. I had wende surer I shulde you have founde.
>   He that trusteth in his strength
>   She him deceyveth at the length.

Bothe strength and beaute forsaketh me.
Yet they promysed me fayre and lovyngly.

(ll. 819–30)

Rex Vivus had occasion to realize the same deception in Strength and Health, and from this other version of the coming of death it seems likely that he spoke in the manner of Everyman of his error in having heeded their flattery in the first place.

The likelihood is considerably reinforced by comparison with the death of Mankynde in *The Castell of Perseverance*.[11] This play and *The Pride of Life*, closely contemporary, are the two oldest of the English moral plays, the only two of certain English origin that feature the character Death, and the only two that trace the experience of the soul after its separation from the body. Moreover, in them Death strikes the hero dead and does not merely issue God's summons. The dying Mankynde is quickly and painfully disabused of his trust in his supposed friend the World much as Everyman is disabused about Strength or, earlier, about Worldly Goods, but here the action continues and resolves itself in a manner that calls to mind the outline in the Prologue to *The Pride of Life*. Soul and Body become separate characters, though their dispute is only incipient. A fiend in the shape of Mankynde's Malus Angelus carts the Soul toward Hell, but he is saved by divine intercession—not, it is true, by Our Lady but by Peace and Mercy, daughters of God who debate before their Father against their sisters Justice and Truth as Our Lady must have argued for the soul of the King of Life. This would seem a more elaborate resolution than that described for *The Pride of Life*, in which the soul finds salvation "through priere of oure lady mylde." But a curious link between these two primitive plays suggests that they did treat the aftermath of death similarly, in fact that at one time, or in one form, the *Castell* play was resolved by the same divine agency as was *The Pride of Life*. The *Castell* play also has a prologue, or Proclamation, spoken by two flagbearers several days before the performance so as to advertise the play in the town where it was next to be performed. The Proclamation contains a summary of the plot. It falls to Primus Vexillator to describe the salvation of

the Soul. Saying nothing about the Daughters of God, he instead
declares that when a man is dead and the Bad Angel claims his
soul it will nonetheless reach Purgatory "& oure lofly lady, if sche
wyl for hym mell" (l. 124). Our Lady is not a character in the
Castell play as we have it. The Proclamation thus offers presumptive
evidence that in some variant of the full scope play, or in such another play, the coming of death was resolved in the same simple
manner as it was in *The Pride of Life* and that what we now have
in the *Castell* drama is an elaboration upon the same essential idea
as governed the spiritual destiny of the King of Life.

Struck to the heart by Death's lance, Mankynde turns instinctively
(l. 2853) to his old friend the World: "helpe now Mankend!"
Mundus replies with the same illuminating sarcasm as Strength and
Worldly Goods directed to Everyman: "Owe, Mankynd, hathe
Dethe wyth the spoke?" He wishes Mankynde "in the erthe beloke,"
in the "colde clay." In the last moments of his life Mankynde is thus
radically disabused of his faith in the World. He wishes it woe and
draws for the good men of the audience the moral of his tragic
experience:

> He beryth a tenynge tungge.
> Whyl I leyd with hym my lott,
> Ye seyn whou fayre he me behott;
> And now he wolde I were a clott,
>   In colde cley for to clynge.
>   (ll. 2890–94)

Similarly, Rex Vivus has laid his lot with Strength and Health, and
they have spoke him fair. Certainly in the lost part of the play he
perceived that they were vanity.

The preliminary shock of recognition occasioned by the failure of
Strength and Health dissolved, no doubt, into the King's full realization of the implications of his plight in the scene following, in which
according to the Prologue (l. 100) "The soule & body schul dispyte."
This episode must have resembled *The Desputisoun bitwen the Bodi
and the Soule,* extant in several versions written between 1300 and
1450. Like all such poems, this one is an exchange of recriminations,

each participant pointing out to the other what he should have realized in life. The soul, Anima, first of all accuses the body of undue regard for pomp and pride, of favoring the rich and disregarding houseless poverty. The Bishop, in the monologue of social criticism which he delivers from his seat before being called to counsel Rex Vivus, introduces the theme into the play, and so it is doubly likely to have figured in the King's tragic realization. It is a theme connected as well with the deaths of both Everyman and Mankynde. Anima declares,

> For to bere thi word ful wide,
> And make of the rime and raf,
> Riche men for pamp and pride
> Largeliche of thine thou gaf.
> the pouer yede al bi side,
> Ever thou hem overhaf;
> And yif thai com in thine unride,
> Thai were ystriken with a staf.[12]

The Body acknowledges that he shall rot even as Alexander and imperial Caesar. They were warned, says Anima, in what would readily become, in the play, a reference to Queen and Bishop, but "Litel hede tok thou of that." The Body counters that the Soul should have restrained him; instead the blind led the blind. The Soul weeps and accuses the Body anew. The Body tries to pray. The Soul sees "fendes" coming to fetch it off to Hell. It is a clear parallel to the corresponding action reported in the Prologue to the play:

> Qwhen the body is doun i broght
> the soule sorow a wakith;
> the bodyis pride is dere a boght:
> the soule the ffendis takith. (ll. 93–96)

In the *Desputisoun* the Soul cries to Jesu for mercy at the brink of Hell, but the vision ends with a terrifyingly realistic account of its damnation. In *The Pride of Life*, however, Our Lady interceded on the Soul's behalf, praying her Son so mild to save the King of Life.

But whether damned or saved, the figure in the *Desputisoun* and the King of Life have achieved the same wisdom.

Since we have had to view the agon and the moral awakening of Rex Vivus indirectly, by reference to the Prologue and to late medieval literature closely akin to *The Pride of Life*, any comparison to the equivalent experience of King Lear must be conjectural and uncertain. This is especially so with respect to details of the story invented by the playwright and not likely to be shared by him with other literature such as I have cited. We cannot know whether Solas, for example, like Lear's Fool accompanied his king into the nightmare of death, though even if he did, his character as revealed earlier in the play hardly promises that he might, with the license of foolery, have chided the folly of his master. Did he ever appear as Earl of Kent, and what became of Queen and Bishop? It would be interesting to know whether the boy playing the Queen doubled parts and played Our Lady in the dénouement, a possibility which would align her yet more strongly with Cordelia, the scorned lady who becomes the agent of restoration. We cannot even be certain that after their candy words Strength and Health turned vicious and destructive toward the King as do Goneril and Regan. (Gloucester knows that Lear's "Daughters seeke his death" and that there is "a plot of death upon him" [III, iv, 168; III, vi, 96.]) The example of World in the *Castell* play and of Goods and Strength himself in *Everyman* argues that Rex Vivus' false friends indeed resembled the pelican daughters in this respect, but perhaps, like Herod's two boastful knights, those of the King of Life failed him quietly in the test and died along with him. But despite these and other uncertainties, the comparison proves an essential kinship between this morality and this tragedy, and in so doing prompts reinterpretation of Lear's experience in the middle portion of the tragedy, in the scenes of the main plot from Act I, scene iv, through Act IV, scene vi. By then suffering has brought the king to a vision of vanity and injustice broader far than the vision called for by the explicit issues of the opening scene. The scenes of realization are secular, actual, concrete. But in Lear's imagination and in the related effects contrived by Shakespeare, in naked Tom and his Foul Fiend, in the symbolic, vanishing knights, in the glimpse of Hell pit and the smell of mortality, for instance— the scenes variously and increasingly project what was allegorical and religious in *The Pride of Life* and increasingly revive the universal religious meaning of that play and *Everyman*.

It is evident from the Prologue and analogues to *The Pride of Life* that tragic realization on the part of the King of Life dominated the play from his encounter with Death to his unexpected and undeserved redemption. He perceived first the uselessness of Strength and Health and perhaps heard their sarcastic farewells as he died. Through the dialogue between his Body and Soul he must have come to understand yet more fully than through death alone the truth of what Queen and Bishop had told him. Presumably he repented of his violence toward his loving queen. Judging from the Bishop's monologue on the tyranny of the wealthy and from the recurrence of the same motive in the *Desputisoun*, as well as from other evidence, it seems most probable that the King's growing insight included awareness of the economic injustice of his reign, even though this theme was not made explicit in his own behavior in the extant section of the play proper. After the fiends had gripped him he quite certainly caught his glimpse of Hell—presumably at the northern scaffold of the theater as in the *Castell* play. By the time Our Lady noticed him and interceded with Christ in his behalf, his chastened spirit would have recognized, with that of Mankynde in the parallel ending of the *Castell* play, that his former worldly vanity was a form of madness.

All this has its equivalent in *King Lear*. Lear too first of all discovers the worthlessness of his two flatterers. His awakening proceeds beyond increasingly profound understanding of his family and himself to embrace a realization of his hitherto inadequate concern for the plight of loop'd and window'd raggedness. On the heath he rashly challenges and contends with, not death, but the fretful elements, and though of course he does not yet literally die, in his mind he supposes that he is dead and bound in Hell upon a wheel of fire. There, just before sanity returns, he further imagines that he is looked upon by a soul in bliss and his body taken from the grave. In the tempestuous middle section of the action Lear exchanges wrath for shame and humility, and kingship for self-knowledge and communion with Cordelia. Before he is bound upon the wheel of fire, he endures his own, obscene vision of what Malus Angelus in the *Castell* play called "helle pytt." No literal fiends snatch him, but the Foul Fiend is continually present to him through the feigned ravings of Edgar—"Croke not blacke Angell, I have no foode for thee" (III, vi, 32–33)—and Hell, Lear determines (IV, vi), is that part of woman which is "all the Fiends." He sees in Poor Tom (III, iv) who "ow'st the Worme no Silke; the Beast, no Hide; the Sheepe, no Wooll; the Cat, no perfume," what unaccommodated man really is, "a poore, bare, forked Animall." So far from wishing to retain a hundred knights and all the addition of a king, Lear now tries to tear from his body the "Lendings" that made him appear sophisticated. Much of Lear's agon, in short, is best interpreted as a renunciation of worldly vanity, and to the extent that it is so interpreted, his behavior at the outset of the play becomes retrospectively a dramatization of such vanity. It is not, in the end, simply that Lear lacked political wisdom and self-knowledge and in his dotage rashly misjudged his daughters. As the memorable opening scene of the tragedy is placed in retrospect by subsequent scenes of the Lear plot, it is, so to speak, made to imply other dimensions of Lear's initial folly as well. One group of these concerns social, legal, and economic injustice, and Lear's insights here are especially notable because they are of a kind uncommon to Shakespeare which correspond closely to ideas prevalent in a class of medieval literature contemporary with *The Pride of Life*. Another set, despite the celebrated paganism of *King Lear*, involves a strictly Christian eschatological view of human life. It will prove convenient to examine Lear's growing moral awareness somewhat more closely under the headings of vanity, social justice, and the Christian supernatural.

Shakespeare's primary reason for introducing Poor Tom is to provide visual contrast to the king's finery and to motivate Lear's realization of the humble nature of man. The special symbol of vanity is dress, and Lear's change from the royal gown he wore in the opening ceremony in his court to the tatters and fantastical

garlands he wears in Act IV, scene iv, expresses the inner transformation of vanity to humility. Edgar himself, the elder son of an earl,
has come to this near-nakedness. His reason, to escape the persecution
of his misguided father, is less important in the play than the form of
disguise he chooses. Before his metamorphosis, using one of the key,
reiterated words in the tragedy, Edgar observed: "*Edgar* I nothing
am" (II, iii, 21). In part the meaning is that he shall no longer be
Edgar, but the words also say that as Edgar he is nothing, while a
Bedlam beggar, "the basest, and most poorest shape" that ever penury
brought man to, is yet something. This is one of several ways in
which Edgar is identified with Lear, who, as the Fool makes very clear
to him in the Fool's great scene (I, iv) is an O without a figure,
nothing, since he gave all to his daughters. The uses of the term in
King Lear are various and complex, but one of the overtones of
nothing is "vanity." The speeches of Edgar as Poor Tom, like those
of the Fool, are full of moral meaning. In his set of injunctions for
how to escape the Foul Fiend, that is, damnation, he declares, "set not
thy Sweet-heart on proud array. *Tom's* a-cold" (III, iv, 83), and Tom
goes on to describe his past identity, that of a lecherous courtier,
"Proud in heart, and minde," with curled hair and gloves in his cap.
Before he came to misery, Tom later adds (III, iv, 141) he had
"three Suites to his backe, six shirts to his body." In these and
other places in the play, fine clothing is the emblem of vanity and
sinfulness.

Thus there is pertinence as well as incipient madness in Lear's
desire, in immediate response to Tom's speech about his fall from
elegance to fiend-haunted penury, to become as Poor Tom by pulling
off his clothes and so achieve the condition of essential humanity:

> Thou wert better in a Grave, then to answere with thy
> uncover'd body, this extremitie of the Skies. Is man no more
> then this? Consider him well. Thou ow'st the Worme no
> Silke; the Beast, no Hide; the Sheepe, no Wooll; the Cat,
> no perfume. Ha? Here's three on's are sophisticated. Thou
> art the thing it selfe; unaccommodated man, is no more but

such a poore, bare, forked Animall as thou art. Off, off you
Lendings: Come, unbutton heere. (III, iv, 104–13)

In *The True Chronicle History of King Leir*, scene xxiii, Leir
removes his fine gown and exchanges it for one of gabardine so as
to pay his passage to Gallia. The moral relevance which Shakespeare
attaches to a similar act typifies the vast difference between the two
dramatic handlings of the same story and the alignment of *King Lear*
with plays of the coming of death. Lear's vanity in Act I, scene i,
was personal, not yet associated with the question of what man is
in the universe. He tried to stage a public show of what should be
a private matter, love, and wanted to have his ego ceremonially
flattered by his daughters, not really to learn how to divide his kingdom among them. In part, his recognition of this error is also
personal. He learns that two of his daughters were false, and he is
at last content that he and Cordelia should be alone in prison to sing
like birds in a cage and discuss disinterestedly the ebb and flow of
worldly life. But steadily his recognition is generalized to include
all human pomp and pride, all sophistication. His pulling off his
clothes, that is to say, cannot be explained only by his disillusion with
Goneril and Regan. Without introducing allegory, it takes the action
to the universal plane of *Everyman* and *The Pride of Life*. Everyman
was a proud dandy rather like Tom before good fortune deserted
him, and in the agon he scourges himself for it:

> Take this, body, for the synne of the flesshe!
> Also thou delytest to go gay and fresshe,
> And in the way of dampnacyon thou dyd me brynge!
> (ll. 13–15)

The suffering of Rex Vivus was no doubt closer still to that of
Lear. His vanity, explicitly representing that of all proud men, had
like Lear's been attuned to the high voices of flattery, reverberating
hollowness. He too was dressed in the robes of a king, but for the
medieval playwright these were symbolic of vanity from the outset;
they are largely why he made his protagonist a king. When at last the

body's pride was "dere a boght" the vanity of its kingly attire would certainly have been made explicit, in the dispute of Body and Soul if not elsewhere. And the horrifying contrast between the King of Life and the King of Death, the contrast of the death-dance, would have made the point as well. The initial contrast between Lear and Poor Tom in the storm, although Tom is no agent of death, functions like the grim pairing of figures in the *dans macabre*. The Bedlam beggars as Edgar describes them, faces grimed with filth, loins blanketed, hair all elfed in knots, who "with presented nakednesse out-face / The Windes" and

> with roaring voices,
> Strike in their num'd and mortified Armes
> Pins, Wodden-prickes, Nayles, Sprigs of Rosemarie
> (II, iii, 14–16)

offer a "horrible object" (i.e., spectacle) not unlike Lear before Cordelia saves him and not unlike Death in the Hegge cycle, "nakyd and pore of array."

The storm in *King Lear*, as it is created for us by Lear's famous apostrophes to it (III, ii), is such a universal destructive force as is Death in late medieval literature. And like Death it is a great equalizer. In the *Castell* play and the Hegge *Death of Herod* the character Death lays stress upon his ability to subdue Kaiser, Duke, and Earl with the same ease as the basest ranks of humankind. The Dance of Death in all its forms taught that death leveled all ranks, and that is why the king is the most tragic participant in it. It is, as la Muerte says in the Spanish version, a lowly dance. But in the Spanish dance and in the coming of death to Mankynde and Rex Vivus the conflict between proud life and the principle of mortality dramatizes not only the essential equality of men but the corollary of that, the injustice inherent in the social order. Unexpectedly in a playwright dedicated as a rule, and not least in other parts of this very play, to prerogative and an aristocratic ordering of society, the storm teaches this corollary as well.

Lear's first insight after he has left his false daughters and clashed with the elements is into the injustices of rank, and it leads

to an injunction to pomp to "Take Physicke" and so end social and
economic injustice by an equal distribution of wealth. The context
suggests that Lear's critique of the feudal system itself (not only
of its abuses) is the voice of wisdom, as if one were reading
Piers Plowman or More's *Utopia.* Lear insists that the Fool enter the
shelter of the hovel before him and then gives voice to his realization
of the injustice in his realm:

> Poore naked wretches, where so ere you are
> That bide the pelting of this pittilesse storme,
> How shall your House-lesse heads, and unfed sides,
> Your lo[o]p'd, and window'd raggednesse defend you
> From seasons such as these? O I have tane
> Too little care of this: Take Physicke, Pompe,
> Expose thy selfe to feele what wretches feele,
> That thou maist shake the superflux to them,
> And shew the Heavens more just.
>
> (III, iv, 28–36)

Later the blinded Gloucester, finding that his wretchedness makes
Poor Tom relatively happier, echoes and reinforces the idea in
simpler words:

> Heavens deale so still:
> Let the superfluous, and Lust-dieted man,
> That slaves your ordinance, that will not see
> Because he do's not feele, feele your powre quickly:
> So distribution should undoo excesse,
> And each man have enough.   (IV, i, 69–74)

This stress upon the vicious injustice of the rich toward the poor
forms one of the most interesting of the probable links between the
suffering of Lear and Rex Vivus. The Bishop in *The Pride of Life*
puts similar stress upon this inequity. He touches on various disorders
of the world—that truth is gone to the ground, that love is lechery,
that "cildrin bet onlerit," and so forth—but dwells on the rich and
poor:

> yes ricmen bet reuthyles,
> ye por got to ground,
> & fals men bet schanles:
> the sot ic hav i found.
>
> Ye ric kynyt it is wrong
> al, yat ye por dot:
> far yat is sen, day & nit,
> wo sa wol sig sot.
>
> paraventur men halt me a fol
> to sig yat fot tal;
> yai farit as ficis in a pol:
> ye gret eteit ye smal.
>
> ric men spart for noying
> to do ye por wrong;
> yai yingit not on her ending,
> ne on det, yat is so stronge.
>
> (ll. 351–66)

The last two lines connect the proud king with this tyranny, though his wealth is not a theme of the opening scenes, and it is most probable therefore that in his suffering he shared with Lear a new awareness of the plight of poverty in his realm. The likelihood is increased by the analogues. La Muerte found El Rey a tyrant who took "de fazer justicia muy poco curastes" much as Lear took "Too little care." The Soul accuses the Body in the *Desputisoun:*

> Riche men for pamp and pride
> Largeliche of thine thou yaf.
> The pouer yede al bi side,
> Ever thou hem overhaf. . . .

Death himself in *The Castell of Perseverance* equates the avarice of Mankynde with that of a classed society, using the same figure of the fish devouring each other as the Bishop of Rex Vivus used in his long monologue of social criticism: "the grete fyschys ete the smale" (l. 2820).

Thus the two earliest morality-play treatments of death introduce the theme of the economic abuses of greatness which preoccupies Lear, though neither Lear nor Rex Vivus has been characterized at the outset, in his proud behavior, as inconsiderate toward the poor. In both *King Lear* and *The Pride of Life*, the private and familial vanity of the king takes on this social dimension, if we assume that the Bishop's sermon applies to the King. The Bishop's monologue as a whole, beginning with the idea that "dred of god is al ago," notably resembles the opening complaint of God in *Everyman*, which supplies God's motive for sending Death to beset "Every man . . . that liveth beastly." If he leaves such people alone, God muses in *Everyman*,

> Veryly they wyll become moche worse than beestes;
> For now one wold by envy another up ete;
> Charity they do all clene forgete. (ll. 48–50)

Again the notion is of a mutual devouring among men, and it is because they, represented by Everyman, "be so combred with worldly ryches / That nedes on them I must do justyce." It is not overly rash, then, to take for granted that eventually Rex Vivus took on responsibility for the social viciousness of which the Bishop speaks in the surviving fragment. It cannot be shown that he acknowledged responsibility as Lear does, that his enlightened judgment upon Strength and Health was joined by sudden awareness that he had taken too little care of the poor in his realm, but it is not unlikely. Certainly the pervasive bestial imagery in the agon of *King Lear* as well as the stage-image of Poor Tom (in "the basest, and most poorest shape / That ever penury in contempt of man, / Brought neere to beast") and the speeches about disencumbering the rich that Tom inspires in Lear and Gloucester are the Shakespearean equivalent to the Bishop's sermon in *The Pride of Life*. Shakespeare is not so much criticizing Jacobean society as writing a play that belongs to the same family as *The Pride of Life* and *Everyman*. These morality plays on the coming of death, together with the section of the *Castell* play devoted to that event, all tell us in choric passages that society governed by pride is viciously self-destructive, like "beestes" or "ficis in a pol." In its broader and more complex way *King Lear* also tells us this. That "morall foole" the good duke Albany sums up with Shakespearean eloquence the idea more quaintly phrased by the Bishop whom "paraventur men halt . . . a fol" and by God in *Everyman*,

> If that the heavens doe not their visible spirits
> Send quickly downe to tame th[ese] vild offences,
> It will come,
> Humanity must perforce pray on it self,
> Like monsters of the deepe.　(IV, ii, 46–50)

The Christian eschatological theme central to *The Pride of Life* is introduced into the pagan world of *King Lear* by the Foul Fiend who hounds Poor Tom. Virtually Edgar's first words in his disguise are these, "Away, the foule Fiend followes me" (III, iv, 46), and thereafter the Fiend is always on the Bedlam's lips. Indisputably a Christian fiend, and probably to be understood as the Devil himself, Tom's Fiend does not pursue the soul of the protagonist as in the moral play; the relationship is not so simple as that. But as we have noted Tom is in some ways parallel to Lear, and he is vexed now by the Fiend because in his days of elegance he sinned "Proud in heart, and minde." At first sight of him Lear underscores the parallelism: "Did'st thou give all to thy Daughters? And art thou come to this?" And a few lines later: "Ha's Daughters brought him to this passe? Could'st thou save nothing? Would'st thou give 'em all?" The parallel narrows almost to an identity as Lear still continues to cast Tom in his own role:

> 　　　　. . . nothing could have subdu'd Nature
> To such a lownesse, but his unkind Daughters.
> Is it the fashion, that discarded Fathers,
> Should have thus little mercy on their flesh:
> Judicious punishment, 'twas this flesh begot
> Those Pelicane Daughters.　(III, iv, 70–75)

Tom keeps the motif of sin and punishment via the Fiend in the language of the play through this and the next scene (III, vi) of the

Lear plot. It is perhaps the Bedlam's nonsense about Hell which inspires the curious episode (omitted in the Folio text) of the trial of Goneril and Regan. Lear sees a vision of his evil daughters tortured by fiends in Hell—"to have a thousand with red burning spits come hiszing in upon them"—and he quickly determines that "It shal be done, I wil arraigne them straight." It is not, as generally supposed, an ordinary court of law that Lear imagines, but one deciding the issue between grace and damnation. Through the agency of Edgar, the Fiend "stands and glars," the black angel croaks for his food. Had they not vanished, Lear in his mind would have sent his vicious daughters to Hell, and the two judges he appoints to condemn them, yoke fellows in equity, are from the bottom of the social hierarchy, the mad beggar and the Fool. The issue of salvation and damnation is still peripheral to the king himself, but it is a question of growing urgency as we move through the scenes devoted to the agony of Lear toward his restoration at the hands of Cordelia.

After the trial, the exhausted Lear, imagining that he is in his own bed, draws the imaginary curtains and falls asleep. He is borne away to a litter, on the advice of Gloucester, by Kent and the Fool. He does not appear on stage again until, wholly mad and wholly enlightened, fantastically dressed, he has his great scene (IV, vi) with blind Gloucester, who in the meantime has undergone his own complete education in the nature of his two sons and in the relationship of men and the gods. Here, the king speaks the definitive words on the events of the opening scene of the tragedy, and through his final consideration of human injustices arrives at his vision of the human Hell generated by lechery, the "expense of spirit in a waste of shame," as Shakespeare calls it in Sonnet 129.

The moment of Lear's falling asleep, then, corresponds to the moment of the death of the King of Life. Whether the King of Life died in bed we cannot tell; but Mankynde did so in the closest analogue. After he is wounded to the heart by Death, the aged Mankynde turns to the World for aid, who laughs and wishes him dead. "Ow, Werld! Werld evere worthe wo!" Mankynde cries, ". . . he beryth a tenynge tungge." The words find a Shakespearean echo in Edgar's exclamation

> World, World, O world!
> But that thy strange mutations make us hate thee,
> Life would not yeelde to age.
>   (IV, i, 10–12)

Eventually Mankynde lies down on his bed under the Castle, and the part is carried on by Anima, his soul, which is at last snatched from the brink of Hell by the Daughters of God as we know that the soul of Rex Vivus was rescued by Our Lady. Similarly Lear, by the time he falls asleep, has been educated in the vanity of the false things in his life, and he is carried out, later to wander in a limbo till recovered by Cordelia. The moment has an aura of death, for it is here that Gloucester announces, "I have ore-heard a plot of death upon him," and the Fool drops out of the play after remarking, "And Ile go to bed at noone," foreseeing perhaps an untimely grave. Lear's body is returned as it were from sophistication to Nature—

> Crown'd with ranke Fenitar, and furrow weeds,
> With Hardokes, Hemlocke, Nettles, Cuckoo flowres,
> Darnell, and all the idle weedes that grow
> In our sustaining Corne   (IV, iii, 3–6)

—and it is in this condition that he tells Gloucester that his hand "smelles of Mortality" (IV, vi, 136). When Cordelia has at last recovered him, the illusion still lingers in his mind as he looks up at her that he is dead, his body in the grave and his soul in Hell:

> You do me wrong to take me out o'th'grave,
> Thou art a Soule in blisse, but I am bound
> Upon a wheele of fire, that mine owne teares
> Do scal'd, like molten Lead.   (IV, vii, 45–48)

In the scene before this, Lear like the King of Life between his death and salvation is in a position to see truth in the perspective supplied by tragic suffering. The sum of the wisdom he has earned is contained in the utterances of his madness, and he no longer needs Kent, the Fool, or even Edgar to instruct him. Here, in the country-side near Dover, the king makes his definitive statement about the flattery accorded him by Goneril and Regan. Mistaking Gloucester for Goneril with a white beard, he thinks back upon her and her sister Regan who flattered him like a dog, told him he was wise, and said Aye, and No, to everything that he said; but Aye, and No too, "was no good Divinity." They were not men of their words, for they told him he was "every thing" (the antithesis of what the Fool called him soon after), but experience has shown that he is not ague-proof. In having Lear say that the Aye and No was bad theology, Shakespeare is not I think alluding to James 5. 12, usually mentioned in the glosses: "But above all things, my brethren, swear not, neither by heaven, neither by the earth, neither by any other oath: but let your yea be yea; and your nay, nay; lest ye fall into condemnation." The passage has little to do with the peril of swearing. Nor is Lear referring vaguely to the former behavior of his courtiers. With the insight of his madness he is giving theological meaning to the hollow acquiescence of his two wicked daughters in whatever he would say to them. That was no good divinity because it plumed his ego and banished from his mind the knowledge that he was like other men subject to the limitations of mortality, not at all ague-proof. Lear's words do not literally apply to Goneril and Regan in Act I, scene i, but suggest the meaning which their behavior has taken on in the course of the tragedy, meaning much the same as that of Strength and Health in *The Pride of Life*. Rex Vivus could appropriately and quite literally have said the words of King Lear about them.

Lear goes on to describe the state of the world, "how this world goes," as he now recognizes it. His views are much the same as those in the long lament of the Bishop, and indeed Lear himself now feels himself qualified to "preach." "Lov is now al lecuri," the Bishop had said of the world (l. 339), and Lear pardons the adulterer whom he imagines before him, since lechery is ubiquitous. The simpering Dame who minces virtue in fact goes to it with riotous appetite, and such women are women only down to the waist. Through his consideration of lechery King Lear arrives at Hell: "But to the Girdle do the Gods inherit, beneath is all the Fiends. There's hell, there's darkenes, there is the sulphurous pit; burning, scalding, stench, consumption:. Fye, fie fie; pah pah" (IV, vi, 128–31). It is in its own way a view of Hell as terrifying as that in the *Castell* play and the *Desputisoun*, and, no doubt, as the Hell toward which the fiends tried to take the soul of the King of Life. The Bishop in his sermon describes Hell presently, but first he turns to his main theme of injustice, in terms strangely like those now used by Lear. Slothful men are blind, says the Bishop, and high place becomes cruel—

> slot men blet bleynd
> & lokit al amis;
> he becomit onkynd
> & yat is reut, i wis.   (ll. 343–46)

These rich men be ruthless, he adds in a stanza already quoted, and false men are shameless; to the rich knight whatever the poor do is wrong. But in Hell no bail (maynpris) nor writ to stay proceedings (supersidias) avails these false ministers, nor the fact that they be king or judge:

> yer no fallit ne maynpris,
> ne supersidias;
> thayt the be kyng or justis,
> ye passit not ye pas.   (ll. 379–82)

Compare Lear:

> A man may see how this world goes, with no eyes. Looke with thine eares: See how yond Justice railes upon yond simple theefe. Hearke in thine eare: Change places, and handy-dandy, which is the Justice, which is the theefe. . . . Thou, Rascall Beadle, hold thy bloody hand: why dost thou lash that Whore? Strip thy owne backe, thou hotly lusts to use her in that kind, for which thou whip'st her. The usurer hangs the Cozener. Thorough tatter'd cloathes great Vices do appeare: Robes, and Furr'd gownes hide all. . . . Get thee glasse-eyes, and like a scurvy Politician, seeme to see the things thou dost not.   (IV, vi, 153–76)

The lax blindness of magistrates, the bad effect of office on character, and the lack of justice when the rich judge the poor are important

points of contact, and Lear's idea that punisher and punished are
interchangeable in guilt is implicit in what the Bishop has to say.
King Lear has come through his suffering from vanity to the same
critique of the world that is defined as the opinion of wisdom in
The Pride of Life.

Just before he lapses into incoherence and scampers away from
the Gentleman sent by Cordelia, Lear turns from satire toward more
positive and religious philosophy. "Thou must be patient," he tells
poor Gloucester, showing how thoroughly he has changed from the
king of Act I,

> we came crying hither:
> Thou know'st, the first time that we smell the Ayre
> We wawle, and cry. I will preach to thee: Marke.
>   (IV, vi, 182–84)

Life is typified by the tears of birth, and we had best resign ourselves
to that. Had he been able to continue his sermon Lear might have
said what Edgar (V, ii) later tells Gloucester, that "Men must endure / Their going hence, even as their comming hither, / Ripenesse
is all." This is a way of phrasing the central lesson of the old plays
on the coming of death, and Lear's pilgrimage across Britain has
made him ready to be saved.

Restoration

Cordelia, absent from the drama since her appearance in the
opening scene where she spoke forty terse lines, unexpectedly becomes
in Act IV the agent of Lear's restoration to sanity and love. Shakespeare treats her in this act as a saintly figure. Before her actual re-
appearance, the Gentleman describes her compassionate reaction to
the news of Lear's suffering. (The scene is entirely omitted in the
Folio.) She was a queen over her passion though tears trilled down
her delicate cheek. She was moved, but

> Not to a rage, patience and sorow str[ove]
> Who would expresse her goodliest. You have seene,

Sun shine and raine at once, her smiles and teares
Were like a better way[,] those happie smilets,
That playd on her ripe lip seeme[d] not to know,
What guests were in her eyes which parted thence,
As pearles from diamonds dropt.
                                        (IV, iii, 18–24)

She exclaimed against her sisters and "shooke, / The holy water from her heavenly eyes" (IV, iii, 31–32). The scene, though unnecessary to the plot, introduces us to another view of Cordelia than we might hold after her tight-lipped words in Act I. It readies us to see her perform the function of Our Lady Mild at the equivalent point in *The Pride of Life*. In the same scene Kent remarks that a "soveraigne" and "burning" shame detains Lear from Cordelia. Wholly contrite, he is ready for her ministrations.

Shakespeare continues this preparation in the next scene, in which Cordelia reappears on stage. She sends forth a century, a hundred soldiers, to find him, and asks the Doctor, "What can mans wisedom / In the restoring his bereaved Sense?" He prescribes rest, and she prays,

                    All blest Secrets
          All you unpublish'd Vertues of the earth
          Spring with my teares; be aydant, and remediate
          In the good mans distresse. (IV, iv, 15–18)

In the restoration scene itself, she prays again to the "kind Gods" to cure her "childe-changed Father" (IV, vii, 14–17), and the king is carried into her presence dressed in fresh garments and asleep. As music plays she kisses him, saying,

                         restauratian hang
          Thy medicine on my lippes, and let this kisse
          Repaire those violent harmes, that my two Sisters
          Have in thy Reverence made. (IV, vii, 26–29)

When presently he awakens and hears the music and her voice asking "How fares your Majesty?" small wonder that he supposes her to be "a Soule in blisse," a "spirit," and himself a dead man whose body she is taking without warrant from its grave and whose soul is bound upon a wheel of fire. Within the confines of the romantic, secular, and realistic drama Shakespeare could hardly come closer to duplicating the scene of the redemption of the King of Life through the prayers of Our Lady.

That scene in the moral play was presumably simple, sufficiently implicit in the few words of the Prologue that we can visualize it. Through "priere of oure lady mylde," the Prologue states, "al godenisse scho wol qwyte," and when the fiends have caught the Soul "oure lady schal ther for preye, / so that with her he schal be lafte." There is no reason to doubt that he was left with her, for until Elizabethan times the moral plays always end happily, and Mankynde's soul was redeemed similarly in the contemporary *Castell* play. Perhaps we may gain some further notion of the ending of *The Pride of Life* from the extant poem on the same resolution of a soul's dilemma in several fifteenth-century manuscripts:

> DEATH. I have the soghte many a day,
> for to tak the to my prai.
> In hele thou might have takyne hede
> thus what in ilk man. . . .
> DEVIL. This saule i chalange for to wyne
> that i knaw is ful of syne.
> SOUL. O hope in dede thou help me:
> Godes moder i pray the.
> GUARDIAN ANGEL. All if this saule synnede have;
> oft times forgifnes he gunne crave.
> MARY. For this thou souke in thi childehede;
> sone forgife him his misdede.
> JESUS. I pray the fader graunte thi sonne;
> for my sake mi moder bone.
> GOD. Sone als thou biddes it sall be;
> na thinge will i deny the.[13]

But from the many touches of feeling and characterization in the scenes which are preserved, it seems likely that the playwright handled the salvation of Rex Vivus less perfunctorily than this.

The scene of Lear's "restauratian" closes Act IV. It brings him out of his own dreadful dream of mortality, the Fiend, the sulfurous pit, and the wheel of fire and returns him to reality and to human-kind a changed and humbled man. He perceives that the Lady to whom he finds himself kneeling is simply his child Cordelia. He knows himself, no longer slenderly, but well—"I am a very foolish fond old man, / Fourescore and upward. . . . I am old and foolish"— and speaks no more with the voice of pride. This is the point in *King Lear* corresponding to the end of the action of *The Pride of Life*, the secular equivalent to the King of Life's spiritual redemption through prayer of Our Lady. Act V, then, from the point of view of the primitive moral drama, is an addition to an already completed action, an addition moreover that radically alters the dramatic effect and implicit meaning of that action. Dropping the overtones of a soul's experience sounded so strongly in the agon and restoration, it resumes the purer tone of literal drama. Lear, protagonist of a Jacobean tragedy, must die an actual death beyond the symbolic death of his vain self suffered in the agon; to this event and to the death of Cordelia, now that she is no more than his daughter, *The Pride of Life* is irrelevant. The complex issues of the subplot assert themselves and demand to be resolved; indeed, the subplot precipitates the catastrophe appended to the main plot. Only Lear's few words to Cordelia while she still lives resonate with meaning paralleled in *The Pride of Life*. It makes no difference to him whether they are in prison if he has her. They'll sing and pray and laugh and talk with angelic detachment of court news,

> Who looses, and who wins; who's in, who's out;
> And take upon's the mystery of things,
> As if we were Gods spies: And wee'l weare out
> In a wall'd prison, packs and sects of great ones,
> That ebbe and flow by th'Moone.
>
> (V, iii, 15–19)

Love is private and not for show, the vicissitudes of human pretension to greatness are only occasions for pastime during the mutual con-templation fed by love. Unworldliness and union with Cordelia replace the Christian otherworldliness of the medieval dramatist as the play's ultimate value. So far, as Farnham remarks, it is *as though* during the play "Lear loses the world only to save his soul by confession and penitence. At the end he wants the pomp of kingship no more."[14] But immediately the bastard Machiavel orders them slain in prison, and the sublunary forces of inhumanity and blind casualty take control of them with a vengeance. Here comparison with the corresponding form of medieval drama ceases to illuminate. The Shakespearean avatar of the form of *The Pride of Life* yields the supreme tragedy of pride. That form can tell us nothing about the more terrifying and modern tragedy of humility.[15]

CHAPTER VI

The Uniqueness
of Othello, Macbeth, *and* King Lear

> Let every man in mankind's frailty
> Consider his last day; and let none
> Presume on his good fortune until he find
> Life, at his death, a memory without pain.
> —*Oedipus* (Fitts-Fitzgerald)

In the age of Shakespeare, only his own three, early Jacobean tragedies of a man's misjudgment and bitter realization of it in the Christian universe revive the original forms of English theological drama, the designs of temptation and the coming of death. Shakespeare alone, and only in *Othello* and *Macbeth*, brings the literal and secular drama of his age into intimate touch with the forms of Mankynde's temptation which we know directly only from the Macro MSS. He thus renews, greatly extends, and artistically vindicates the tentative ventures in this direction of amateurs like John Phillip and W. Wager with works to which theirs compare as Peter Quince's "Pyramus and Thisbe" to *Romeo and Juliet*. Almost simultaneously (all within the period 1604–1606) he achieves in *King Lear* a like transmutation into tragedy of the kindred form of the coming of death latent since *The Pride of Life* and *Everyman*, no Tudor playwright, to our knowledge, having tried to renew it. In consequence, these three are also the most Aristotelian among the tragedies of Shakespeare and his contemporaries, uniquely animated by plots in which a Christian peripeteia and anagnorisis (the "recognycion" of the Macro play *Wisdom*) are of the essence.

Othello and *Macbeth* as antitypes of the old temptation dramas stand in the sharpest contrast to a variegated background of dramatic activity in which the structure of the temptation plot practically never survives intact. Least of all is it visible in the other work of major playwrights, including Shakespeare himself. The closer and more widespread affinities to the theological play appear in the minor homiletic drama between 1590 and 1610, but even here the actual pattern of Mankynde's life survives most rarely if at all. Madeleine Doran, concurring with Henry H. Adams and Alfred Harbage, speaks of "the ethical pattern of temptation, sin, repentance, and punishment that domestic tragedy inherited from the morality play,"[1] and Hardin Craig similarly declares, "The pattern of crime in Elizabethan drama was obviously the same as that in the moral play: temptation, sin, discovery, repentance, punishment, and hope of salvation."[2] Though one hesitates to qualify the unanimous opinion of such authorities, the domestic tragedies in my opinion lack the implied actual resemblance to English temptation plays and continuity with them. The ethical pattern is somewhat the same because it is Christian, not because of anything to do with English moral drama.

Much the same may be said of the class of didactic plays that the Elizabethans called "morals," such as the Lodge-Greene *A Looking Glasse for London and England*.[3]

Two Elizabethan plays have been regarded as great reenactments of the native temptation play. The first of these is Marlowe's *The Tragicall Historie of Doctor Faustus*, written between 1589 and 1593 but extant in two difficult and differing editions of 1604 and 1616. *Doctor Faustus*, I believe, is a tragedy fundamentally alien in spirit and design to the family of *The Castell of Perseverance* though Marlowe, most notably in the version reflected by the text of 1616, intuited the possibility of making high tragedy out of the temptation play. Second stands Shakespeare's own *King Henry the Fourth*, in two parts, dating from about 1598. These plays and the subsequent *Henry V* surely owe their pattern of alternating serious and low-comic scenes largely to the development of such a pattern in early Elizabethan hybrids of the morality play like *Cambises*, though on another side it is traceable as far back as Medwall's *Fulgens and Lucres* (ca. 1497). The conception of the young protagonist Prince Hal clearly owes something to the Tudor "youth" plays in the native tradition and even more to Christian Terence drama, by origin Continental but soon anglicized, that made neo-Roman comedy of the career of a prodigal son. Shakespeare here as elsewhere deals far more freely with his raw materials than his fellow dramatists typically do. He tampers artistically with time sequences, for example, and invents out of nothing in history the illuminating contrast of Hal and Hotspur. But notwithstanding that his greatest invention of all is mockingly called a Vice and a misleader of youth, the relationship of *Henry IV* to Tudor drama of temptation is little more than allusive. As for the phases of Mankynde's experience in such drama, not one of them survives in the career of Prince Hal. As soon as we can look below the level of archaism and allusion we shall find *Macbeth* more closely akin to *The Castell of Perseverance* and *Othello* to *A Morality of Wisdom* than are *Doctor Faustus* and *Henry IV* to any specimens of English moral drama.

Yet historians of that drama still trace it as far as *Doctor Faustus* and no farther, which they regard as at once its culmination and the proof of what the idea of the native moral play could amount to, falling at the last into the hands of a great poet.[4] It is true that in *Doctor Faustus* several elements of the temptation play recur, and that they operate for the first time in a genuinely poetical Elizabethan tragedy and one, moreover, of cosmic scope like that of *The Castell of Perseverance.* Lucifer, the Good and Bad Angels who accompany each man through life, and the universal Seven Deadly Sins had not appeared together in any other known play since the great *Castell* play, and these figures help to give *Doctor Faustus* its unusually medieval and theological quality among the Elizabethan tragedies. Hell strives with Grace for conquest in the breast of Faustus as in Mankynde, and at times, particularly toward the end of the tragedy and in the "B" text of the second edition of 1616, Marlowe's lines recall the traditional design of temptation, sin, and recognition. Faustus' exclamation to Mephostophilis—"O thou bewitching fiend, 'twas thy temptation, / Hath rob'd me of eternall happinesse" (ll. 1986–87)[5]—seems both to echo the Mankynde-figures of pre-Elizabethan drama and to anticipate Othello's recognition of the true nature of Iago. These and other echoes and vestiges of English theological drama in *Doctor Faustus* go far toward proving Marlowe's familiarity with that drama and, therefore, its accessibility to contemporary playwrights including Shakespeare. But to the fundamental plan of Marlowe's tragedy they are superficial and even alien or ill-considered. That plan, as W. W. Greg remarks, is of a man who willfully seeks his own destruction.

The temptation plot, broached in its full scope form in the *Castell* play, made more efficient and compact in *Wisdom*, and reenacted in a score of later plays still extant, regularly introduced its protagonist in a state of innocence or of virtue, however susceptible. How else could he offer a fit subject for delusion by the agent of darkness, and how else could a rational creature sin but in delusion? The temptation scene also required as preparation an introduction of this agent, who in counsel with others or in soliloquy might reveal his true nature, hidden from the protagonist, and his strategy. The scene itself, frequently the third scene as it is in *Wisdom*, saw the blinding of the human protagonist to moral truth by equivocation or specious reasoning and a corresponding release of his worse nature from the control of his rational faculties. His sinful acts (in one line of protagonists running from Mankynde to Macbeth) were undertaken in the belief that evil was somehow necessary to his own good, or (in another line from Mankynde in *Wisdom* to Othello) that evil was not evil but good. The only satisfactory resolution of such a plot must originate in a scene of recognition, bitter and salutary, that would undo the work of the tempter and make the protagonist eligible for reinstatement, at the same time releasing the pent-up feelings of the audience who knew all along that he was deceived. The religious plays themselves and all Tudor temptation plays until 1558 involve such a climactic scene of realization. For the early-Elizabethan playwrights who sought to adapt the temptation plot to tragedy, the fundamental problem, in theory at least, was how to reconcile this saving experience with catastrophe. They never solved it, and perhaps it is partly for this reason that the Elizabethan temptation-tragedies are early and few.

Doctor Faustus is related to the temptation plays not so much by its archaisms as by the moral struggle in Faustus' soul. But what the Chorus calls the "forme," that is the design, "of *Faustus* fortunes, good or bad" (l. 9) corresponds hardly at all to the traditional design derived from Mankynde's experience. The sense of the Chorus that he must

> speake for *Faustus* in his infancie.
> Now is he borne, of parents base of stocke,
> In *Germany* . . .   (ll. 11–13)

may be a faint holdover from the old full scope plays. But the man whom we encounter in his study at the outset of the tragedy proper is no exemplar of baptismal innocence. Already

> He surfets upon cursed Necromancie:
> Nothing so sweet as Magicke is to him;
> Which he preferres before his chiefest blisse,
>   (ll. 26–28)

—that is, the salvation of his soul. In his full-blown pride, logic seems to him unworthy of his wit, and his accomplishments in physic leave him "still but *Faustus*, and a man." Law is altogether too servile and illiberal for him. He is determined to transgress the ordinary human limits of power and "get a Deity" through black magic. The bitter syllogism by which he deduces from the Vulgate that we must all sin and be damned (ll. 69–78) is perhaps intended to reveal an accompanying ignorance of the simplest Christian truth, for all his show of being a divine. It betrays the same fatal literalism that finally prevents Faustus from harkening to the scholars and the Old Man and repenting. Whether the conception be credited to Marlowe or to his source, such continuity of spiritual condition is foreign to the ordered but radically varying phases of Mankynde's progress between Heaven and Hell.

Since Faustus' life is damnable from the outset, the scene of conspiracy and the temptation itself of the English moral plays have no place in his tragedy. Faustus himself is the spring of the action. Since he deliberately and consciously sends for them—Valdes and Cornelius and, later, Mephostophilis—the agents of evil hardly need plot against him or lie in wait for him. And since Faustus is already self-deluded, their role, despite his later accusation of Mephostophilis, is truly to serve him in the matter of getting himself damned rather than to tempt him. "How pliant is this Mephostophilis! / Full of obedience and humility" (ll. 257–58)—and not only in the matter of dress to which Faustus refers. When invoked by Faustus, he unambiguously appears in his own ugly devil's shape, and it is Faustus who tells him to exchange that for the "holy shape" of a Franciscan. This is the very inversion of the time-honored technique of tempters in the moral drama of deceiving the protagonist with an honest exterior. Mephostophilis is always open and frank. He speaks eloquently of his torment in being deprived of everlasting bliss and begs Faustus to cease his frivolous questions about Hell, while Faustus takes the sophist's line, confounding Hell in Elysium, dismissing "these vaine trifles of mens soules," and scorning the joys he never shall possess. Mephostophilis' directness makes of him one of Marlowe's unforgettable characters. It also distinguishes him from the devils, sins, and the Vice who deceived the Mankynde-hero of the moral plays and in exactly the same way from Iago and the Weird Sisters.

The midnight signing of the deed of gift of body and soul constitutes Faustus' formal commitment to evil as a way of life. It best corresponds to the moment of moral choice in temptation plays which at once completed the temptation and inaugurated the phase of sin, and it is not achieved without a soul-struggle. Awaiting Mephostophilis' return from Hell, Faustus for a moment hesitates. "Why waverst thou?" (l. 396) he asks himself, setting the possibility of salvation against his appetite for wealth somewhat as Mankynde had done. Marlowe supplements the soliloquy with the second appearance of the Good and Bad Angels, externalizing the inner struggle in the manner of allegorical and hybrid drama. There are further manifestations of heavenly resistance to the signing beyond Faustus' thoughts of salvation and contrition and the projecting of the Good Angel: his blood at first refuses to flow for the writing of the deed, and even when it is completed he sees upon his arm an inscription, which we must assume to be divinely caused, reading "*Homo fuge*," though he is a man too weak or corrupted to fly from evil. Hereupon occurs an interesting stage parallel to the *Castell* play and possible echo of it. Mephostophilis fetches devils who, according to the stage direction, give "Crownes and rich apparell to Faustus" and then dance and depart. We recall that after Malus Angelus brought Mankynde to the world, Mundus clothed him in "ryche aray" before turning him over to Coveytyse and the other Deadly Sins. The scene contains one or two possible allusions to the traditional temptation scenes: Faustus asks whether it is to enlarge his kingdom that Lucifer "tempts us thus" (l. 429), and Mephostophilis to our surprise speaks (l. 461) what sounds like a tempter's aside to the audience: "What will not I do to obtaine his soule?"

Yet, like several passages in the tragedy, this remark is notably inconsistent with the real meaning of the action. Mephostophilis has said nothing disingenuous to Faustus, and all that he has done is to bring the chafer of coals to warm the blood—even this, we note (ll. 454–56), being unnecessary. To our knowledge Lucifer has not tempted Faustus at all. The issue here is radically different from that in any temptation scene: not whether Faustus will turn, deluded, from grace, but whether he will persevere in his own, well-established determination to exchange his soul for power and pleasure. Thus the Bad Angel need not try through sophistry to convert Faustus but only repeats verbatim his earlier injunction, "Go forward *Faustus* in that famous Art" (l. 403). The contract established between Faustus and Lucifer, unlike the arrangements between such protagonists as Mankynde and Macbeth and the powers of darkness, is unequivocal. Faustus writes it out himself, stipulating the terms and conditions which he had originally proposed and submitted, via Mephostophilis, to Lucifer for approval. The scene of the signing of the Deed of Gift is not pivotal like a temptation scene but confirmatory.

The spiritual condition of Faustus during the whole course of the tragedy does not essentially change. Always the godly side of his nature is suppressed, for all its recurrent efforts to gain control. There is no phase of the action during which it is supreme. The inevitable result of his spiritual state is eventual despair and then, when his time is up, disintegration. Faustus lives perpetually the life without faith to which Worldly Man and Philologus, his nearest relatives in Elizabethan drama, descended through the influence of evil forces, and like theirs his heart becomes adamant to Christian admonition. But during the twenty-four years of his life of active transgression, unlike Mankynde, unlike Worldly Man and Philologus, unlike Othello and Macbeth during the equivalent phase of active sin, Faustus on the whole enjoys himself immensely; the powers of Hell fulfill their part of the bargain. On occasion, briefly, during these years Faustus thinks of trying to save himself, and the pair of angels rejoin him, but except for these moments he takes delight in sin. He has no speech corresponding to those in which Macbeth perceives the hollowness and futility of his way of life not only with respect to eternity but in the here and now as well. Only once, on the last night, does he approximate such perception, telling the scholars that "for the vaine pleasure of foure and twenty yeares hath *Faustus* lost eternall joy and felicitie" (ll. 1959–60). The horseplay to which he descends (especially in the longer text of 1616) may seem to us not worth the price of it, and doubtless the purpose of the comic intervals is to parody the greater sins of Faustus, to make evil appear absurd as well as fearful, as David M. Bevington claims.[6] But Faustus finds evil sweet to his Renaissance taste (ll. 595–96): "Have not I made blind *Homer* sing to me / Of *Alexanders* love, and *Oenons* death?" And he takes frank delight in his pranks and in the seven, no longer deadly, sins. Since evil has perpetrated no diabolical deception of Faustus, we the audience feel none of the tension coming from our own superior knowledge that is felt during a temptation play (and that is so especially strong in *Othello*), except insofar as the Good Angel, the scholars, and finally the Old Man convince us that Faustus could truly repent if he would, and so be bathed in grace. Since he has not been juggled with, as have Othello and Macbeth by this stage of the action, Faustus has in store for him no shock of tragic realization. If he was self-deluded on the question of his eligibility for grace (Marlowe is not perhaps entirely clear on the point) Faustus dies so.

The fundamental conception and design of *The Tragicall Historie of Doctor Faustus* come, not from English allegorical drama at all, but from Marlowe's literary source. Marlowe worked from a prose account, much longer than his play, *The Historie of the damnable*

life, and deserved death of Doctor John Faustus (1592), translated
from the German by one P. F., Gent.[7] Marlowe omits a good deal,
and he adds Valdes and Cornelius and the pair of antithetical angels.
Otherwise he depends heavily upon his source, throughout the play
drawing from it the details and scheme of a life consistently damnable,
the episodes and their sequence, even the pattern for alternating the
tragic with the absurd. Unlike all the early Elizabethan playwrights
who had tried to adapt the temptation plot to tragedy and to the
experience of a concrete individual, Marlowe does not refashion the
early episodes of his book to the received dramatic pattern. In this
regard he is considerably less free with his authority than the in-
competent Woodes. To make a play out of Aglionby's account of
Francis Spira, Woodes felt it necessary to stress the Protestant virtue
of Philologus-Spira, however flawed by a propensity for empty talk,
in a scene invented for the purpose, and Woodes leaves Aglionby
altogether in order to show the Catholic tempters planning how to
convert Philologus. He proceeds with a temptation scene of some
six hundred lines culminating in a truly pivotal decision on the part
of the tragic central figure: "My former follyes"—i.e., Protestantism
—"I utterly renownce." Marlowe makes no corresponding effort. It
is not the English temptation play but rather the *Damnable life, and
deserved death of Doctor John Faustus* that he has raised to the level
of poetical tragedy.

And yet, as W. W. Greg was first to point out, Marlowe in the
version of the tragedy represented by the text of 1616 began to think
of Faustus as a man ensnared by Lucifer and Mephostophilis, however inconsistent the notion was with the body of the tragedy. The
most striking evidence for this shift is a passage that occurs just
after the two appearances of Helen of Troy and the admonition of the
Old Man and the Scholars. It is here that Faustus cries out to
Mephostophilis in the lines already cited, "O thou bewitching fiend,
'twas thy temptation, / Hath rob'd me of eternall happinesse." This
accusation, almost in the voice of Macbeth or Othello disabused, is
unjust in terms of the beginning of the play as we have it. Yet, to
our surprise, Mephostophilis replies:

I doe confesse it Faustus, and rejoyce;
'Twas I, that when thou wer't i'the way to Heaven,
Damb'd up thy passage, when thou took'st the booke,
To view the Scriptures, then I turn'd the leaves
And led thine eye.
What weep'st thou? 'tis too late, despaire. . . .

(ll. 1888–93)

These are not the accents of the Mephostophilis of earlier scenes, and this passage looks very much like an effort to rethink Faustus' reading of the Vulgate during his opening monologue retrospectively in terms of devilish trickery practised upon him. As Greg remarks, the apparently chance collocation of scriptural texts there was the immediate cause of Faustus' revolt from God.[8] Mephostophilis was not even present, but the words just quoted suggest how the drama might have been conceived as a tragedy of temptation with Faustus ready to lodge himself with Divinity as after all best and then tricked through specious logic into forsaking God.

Only if Faustus had been thus misled at the outset, or in the conjuration scene, would his epithet "bewitching fiend" be justified. It echoes Mankynde's dying disillusionment in the World as well as anticipates Macbeth's realization that his supernatural solicitors were "Jugling Fiends." It smacks of realization "too late" in the face of catastrophe physical and spiritual, something which no Elizabethan dramatist had hitherto imagined. The exchange is followed by the last and longest appearance of the Good and Bad Angels, still unique to the text of 1616, in which Mephostophilis' idea of "too late" is driven home by both and in which the Bad Angel, exactly like the Malus Angelus of Mankynde, gloatingly invites the doomed protagonist to stare with horror into Hell. Marlowe has turned Elizabethan tragedy back to that combination of realization and catastrophe which the *Castell* playwright had achieved in the death of Mankynde (though in Heaven he annulled the catastrophe) and which the moral drama had never again achieved, always letting recognition lead through regeneration to restoration, or else, in a few Elizabethan morality-tragedies, cancelling the recognition. But the passage in which Marlowe does this (ll. 1983–2034 of the text of 1616) is alien to the rest of the tragedy.

What originally followed in the manuscript lying behind the text of 1616 we do not know; it was perhaps an injunction like that of Mankynde and Macbeth not to act upon the specious promptings of devils. For Greg has shown that the editors of the 1616 text here abandoned their copy and replaced whatever it had supplied with Faustus' great final speech, which they took from the text of 1604. This soliloquy is indeed "wholly out of keeping with the 'morality' element, and . . . irreconcilable with such a conception," as Greg maintains.[9] But it is a fitting period to the dramatic history of a damnable life. To teach through terror the consequences of practicing more than heavenly power permits does not require that the transgression be extenuated by showing it to follow bewitchment by a fiend. Nor does the dramatic effect of the "hellish fall" require to be offset by any renewal of the hero's noble virtue now that he is free, though too late, of fiendish influence. So in the more consistent A text of 1604 the recognition scene is excised, along with certain earlier parallels to the temptation plays like the appearance of Lucifer and Mephostophilis "above" as if on the *sedes* of the *Castell* theater. Without any suggestion that Mephostophilis was a bewitching fiend or any last appearance of the angels to drive home the truth now that it is too late, the 1604 text proceeds directly from the exeunt of the scholars to the last soliloquy. One must not mistake Marlowe's eloquence here for signs of tragic elevation or resolve in Faustus. The final note is of the fearful disintegration of panic: "Ile burne my bookes——." In the sixteenth century such negative examples as the deaths of Apius and Cambises, simple mirrors for magistrates, and of Francis Spira and John Faustus, men doomed by lack of faith, were never made congenial to the design of Mankynde's temptation inherited from pre-Elizabethan days. That design undergoes its tragic apotheosis rather in *Othello* and *Macbeth*.

The play of Shakespeare most frequently linked to the tradition of moral drama is not one of these tragedies, however, but *Henry IV*.

"Holinshed-history," writes A. P. Rossiter, has herein ". . . been patterned according to something which is outside the chronicle," this being "the *Cambises* form" which in Shakespeare's treatment yields "a design, the key-word to which is Honour" and a theme which may be regarded as "entirely abstract and even moral."[10] Bevington has since argued that Parts I and II derive their use of low-comic material, carried forward in alternate scenes with the main plot and mirroring its serious theme, from an early Elizabethan permutation of the morality play. This was caused, he believes, by the need to suppress groups of characters so as to satisfy "the desire to crowd the stage with incident and spectacle, under the limiting conditions of troupe presentation."[11] In Shakespeare the resulting structure survives the need more plainly I should say than it survives in Marlowe, to whom Bevington is chiefly concerned to trace it. *Henry IV* does look like a magnificent extension of a relatively late form taken by English moral drama; this not at all to say that it takes on the form of Mankynde's experience.

The claim that comic scenes invented by early Elizabethans like Thomas Preston "are a secular adaptation of vicious intrigue in the Psychomachia" and a step toward the fully realized subplot in *Henry IV* must be qualified, however, in view of the sophisticated uses of the subplot so much earlier in Henry Medwall's *Fulgens and Lucres*.[12] As will appear, there is good reason to suppose that Shakespeare knew both of Medwall's plays. Here, in an interlude presented at the close of the fifteenth century sixty years before *Cambises* and quite unrelated to the religious allegorical drama, comic action already parallels and mocks the serious. The scene in which two lively Tudor lads vie for the hand of Jone the maid in singing, wrestling, and tilting is proleptic parody of the climactic scene of the main plot in which Gayus and Cornelius compete for Lucres like the parody of the central scene in *1 Henry IV* (III, ii) conducted at the Boarshead Tavern (II, iv).

The mere fact that the theme of *1 Henry IV* may be reduced to abstract terms is hardly evidence of the play's relationship to the mode of English drama distinguished originally by abstraction of human individual experience. Rossiter's assertion that Shakespeare

reshapes chronicle history to achieve a design keyed to honor is not
to be gainsaid. But the artistry by which Hotspur, "the Theame of
Honors tongue," is contrasted to Prince Hal who knows the politic
uses of dishonor for a time, and both young men of Shakespeare's
manufacture to Falstaff, the very incarnation of dishonor, owes after
all rather little to any variant of the traditional allegory of Mankynde.
It is equally bad logic to maintain that the moral bent of the play
associates it with that main line of English plays that we have chosen
to call the moral drama, but in any case the moralizing is far from
the simplicities of "just reward" sufficient unto the *Cambises* class
of plays. The resolution of *1 Henry IV* would probably have out-
raged Preston, the Gascoigne who designed *The Glasse of Govern-
ment*, even Sir Philip Sidney. If it holds ethical and political meaning at all, the play seems to demonstrate in regard to honor that
Falstaff is right: "Who hath it? He that dy'de a Wednesday." He
lives and thus far thrives, and the course toward greatness seems
to require a well-timed transition from riot and dishonor to martial
valor. Hotspur is food for worms. No, the design of honor in *1 Henry
IV* is peculiarly Shakespeare's, potential only to the slightest degree
in the structural break-up which permitted hybrid drama like *Cambises* to achieve the illusion of a stage bustling with varied life. Hal's
epithets for Falstaff, "a Devill . . . in the likenesse of a fat old man,"
"that reverend Vice, that grey Iniquitie," are merely allusive and
decorative in a way that Othello's "that demy-Divell" is not. As for
the phases of Mankynde's experience disrupted for the plot of
Cambises and like plays, if they were ever in the genealogy of
Henry IV they are, in both parts, obliterated.

It is notable, nevertheless, how frequently the study of *Henry IV*
calls to mind the author of the first Tudor refashioning of the religious temptation play as well as of the oldest secular comedy in
English. In Medwall's two-part *Interlude of Nature* (ca. 1498)[13]
Mankynde twice falls in with a character named Pride, who is a
clear forebear of Falstaff. Like Sir John of *Part 2*, for instance,
Pride requires an unusual quantity of cloth for his short coat and
has a tiny boy serving him as page; he is lecherous and in financial
straits. He can speak in Falstaffian accents of mock remorse:

> On my faith I was very glad
> Of your fyrst acquaintaunce
> And now I forthynk yt utterly
> That ever I knew you fy fy fy.
>
> (I, 989–92)

On his way to war he is made the victim of a practical joke and threatened with the possibility that "every knave wyll the[e] call / a coward to thy face" (II, 874–75). Pride understands that Man the protagonist is "borne to great fortunes" and hopes to share in them by their alliance. He is, as Sensualyte slyly puts it, "radix viciorum. Rote of all vertew," and Spivack has pointed out how strikingly one of his evil extensions, Glotony, in his wish to purvey "A nother botell" lest drink be scarce or unavailable on the way to battle, anticipates Falstaff marching through Warwickshire.[14] Moreover, the two parts into which Medwall divides *Nature*, Mankynde twice disentangling himself from the same Pride and similar attendant low life, adumbrate both parts of *Henry IV* in the very fact of their slightly awkward repetitiveness. Midway in each part Hal turns from Falstaff to more serious pursuits rather as Mankynde had twice left Pride under the influence of Reason. Medwall's moral interlude raises the possibility that Shakespeare may after all have intended from the outset to write *Henry IV* in two parts.

But in his depiction of Falstaff, as in his interrelating of serious and low-comic plots, Shakespeare also imitates the Medwall of *Fulgens and Lucres*. The prototype of those "incomprehensible lyes" which the fat rogue tells at the Boarshead Tavern is the scene in *Fulgens* wherein "A," though in fact he has been thrashed by a girl, entertains Gayus as follows:

> A. They leyd awayte for me in the way
>   And so they lefte me in this araye.
> GAYUS. Ye, but haste thou ony dedely wounde?
>   That is the thinge that feryth my mynde.
> A. I'faythe, I was lefte for dede on the grounde,
>   And I have a grete garce here byhynde. . . .

Here is a man that quyt hym as well
For my defence as ever I see.
He toke suche parte that in the quarell
His arme was strykyne of by the harde kne
And yet he slew of them .ii. or .iii.
GAYUS. Be they slayne? nay, God forbyde!
A. Yes, so helpe me God, I warande them dede.
How be it I stonde in grete drede
That yf ever he come in theyr way
They wyll kyt of his arme or his hede,
For so I herde them all .iii. say.
GAYUS. Whiche? thay that were slayne?
A.   Ye, by this day.
What nedyth me therfore to lye?
He herd it hymselfe as well as I.

                                    (I, ll. 1257-85)

This passage perhaps inspired the scene cited by Spivack in which
John Rastell, who knew *Fulgens* well from having printed it, made
his own contribution toward the later entertainment in Eastcheap:

SENSUAL APPETITE. Gogges nayles, I have payed som of them,
            I tro.
YNGNORAUNCE. Why, man, what eyleth the[e] so to blow?
SENSUAL APPETITE. For I was at a shrewd fray.
YNGNORAUNCE. Hast thou any of them slayn, than?
SENSUAL APPETITE. Ye, I have slayn them every man,
            Save them that ran away.
YNGNORAUNCE. Why, is any of them skapyd and gone?
SENSUAL APPETITE. Ye, by gogges body, everychone,
            All that ever were there.
YNGNORAUNCE. Why than, they be not all slayne.
SENSUAL APPETITE. No, but I have put some to payne,
            For one horeson there was that torned again,
            And streyght I cut of[f] his ere.
YNGNORAUNCE. Than thou hast made hym a cut purse.

SENSUAL APPETITE. Ye, but I servyd another wors!

. . . .

YNGNORAUNCE. Than thou hast quyt the[e] lyke a tal knyght!

Spivack calls our attention to this passage from *The Nature of the Four Elementes* (E₁v-r) as a remarkable instance of Falstaff's genesis in allegorical drama.[15] I quote it again because it exemplifies the kind of modal relationship found between allegorical drama and the tragedies *Othello*, *Macbeth*, and *King Lear*, but with this difference: that in *Henry IV*, though character, dialogue, and situation are borrowed and transmuted into brilliant, literal drama, the plot structure of Mankynde's moral struggle between good and evil is not preserved at all. Indeed, Shakespeare's debt in *Henry IV* seems more directly to Medwall himself, as author of both allegorical and literal comedy, than to theological drama lying behind him. Medwall, as we have noted in Chapter II, retains the essentials of the temptation plot for his moral interlude *Nature*. Mankynde the protagonist is at first in the emblematic company of Innocencye as Prince Hal hardly qualifies to be. Mankynde endures a struggle between his Sensualyte and his Reason, and in the state of sin to which the former introduces him he is truly deluded. It was Medwall, so far as we know, who introduced the use of deceptive names by sins and vices in allegorical drama to "blere the eye" of Mankynde, who thinks he is with Good Felyshyp and Wurship, for example, not with Glotony and Pride. Prince Hal, as we discover in his first scene, is perfectly conscious of the nature of his base companionship ("I know you all, and will a-while uphold / The unyoak'd humor of your idlenesse—"), and it is he who tells us through vivid epithets exactly what Falstaff is. But though he is aptly called "white-bearded Sathan" and "a Devill . . . in the likenesse of a fat old Man," that "reverend Vice" Falstaff is not a Vice in the same sense, that of role, in which Iago may be called a devil in the likeness of an honest man. There is in *Henry IV* no process of temptation, and if either is deluded about the intentions of the other it is Falstaff, not the prince.

Since Hal at the outset (unlike Mankynde) already wastes his substance in riotous living, or appears to, and later comes to his father to reform and be embraced, we may grant, with Dover Wilson, the informing influence of the prodigal son story in *1 Henry IV*, and again in the second part, though the prodigal son was less calculating and aware than Hal and he was the younger son rather than the elder. And it was partly in early Elizabethan prodigal son plays modeled on Continental Christian-Terence drama that the Vice, though retained in the English plays because of his popularity with audiences, lost his opportunity to subvert the protagonist's initial virtue by taking the role of tempter and was left, like Sir John, with essentially nothing to do. The Shakespearean "misleader of Youth" does not really operate upon Hal. The play's relationship to the youth moralities, as to the *Interlude of Nature*, is allusive rather than structural.

It is, in Iago's phrase, a pregnant and unforced position from which one argues the reemergence of the two forms of the English moral play in Shakespeare's first Jacobean tragedies. Having demonstrated in many Tudor plays its potential to inform and give new meaning to literary materials, the tradition of the temptation play, pointing toward Shakespeare though producing nothing of permanent worth since the Macro plays, intersects his career at a logical moment. It does not participate in his earliest plays. *Julius Caesar* and *Hamlet*, early tragedies of Shakespeare's maturity, prefigure a conception of tragedy in which the structures of moral drama might operate. Cassius is not quite a diabolic tempter of flawed Brutus, and Hamlet wrongly suspects that the spirit that he has seen may be the devil, who "hathe power / T'assume a pleasing shape" and who perhaps out of Hamlet's weakness and his melancholy abuses him to damn him. But the passion-flawed nobility of Brutus and Hamlet develops into the truly dual potentiality of character of the central figures in the next tragedies, who will share the stage with subordinate figures correspondingly divided more sharply than elsewhere in Shakespeare into factions of good and evil. Shakespeare, that is, anatomizes human nature both within Othello, Macbeth, Lear and around them in moral contrasts of uncomplex figures as far apart as Hell's from Heaven: Iago and Desdemona, Regan and Cordelia. Here for the first time since the hybrid dramas the design of moral drama can reassert itself. The Moor is the first of Shakespeare's tragic heroes susceptible and rational enough to play Mankynde's role. After a phase of perplexing dark comedy, the dramatist returns to tragedy with *Othello*, a drama of classic economy and clarity, with Iago in the part of human devil. He reworks the career of the legendary Macbeth to make of it another version with different emphasis of linear human experience between evil and good, with three Weird Sisters, who are not, or are not merely, human, cast as instruments of darkness. He causes vain Lear to relive the alternate design for English moral drama, making of Goneril and Regan, not tempters, but those upon whom the human figure depends only to find them utterly false. Regan is "naught," nothing, vanity. The cause in nature that makes her so, Thomas Aquinas would say, is that her human form contains a nonhuman essence; she is alive but soulless. In the Roman heroes of his last, more typically Jacobean tragedies, defects of character, "taints," mingle inseparably with virtues, "honours," in a paradoxical and constant mixture throughout the play. Shakespeare relaxes his pre-occupation with the problem of evil and sets aside the native dramatic forms with which he had stated and investigated it.

I am less convinced that we may see the explanation of Shake-speare's renewal of theological patterns in the age itself, in, say, the "well-defined" Jacobean renewal of medievalism by which Oscar Campbell accounts for the morality-play form of *King Lear*.[16] *Hamlet*, that virtual dance of death, is at least as "medieval" as *Lear*. The private theaters of the time, however, specialized in a kind of sensational negativism and tragic satire, in disillusion that indeed out-Hamlets *Hamlet*, in excesses of the macabre and of barren stoicism, and it may be that such a play as *Othello* is a counterstatement to them. Alfred Harbage has argued persuasively that around the close of the Elizabethan period the impulse to justify the popular dramatic tradition is a motive in Shakespeare's creative life because of com-petition from the coterie playwrights like Marston and Webster.[17] Possibly Shakespeare's reemployment of the dramatic forms, in-evitably Christian, positive, and now humanistic as well in their meaning, is a part of the same reassertion. If, as Harbage puts it, "the impulse to meet aggression by expressing his tradition in works unanswerably good" does motivate Shakespeare after the turn of the century, it is difficult to feel that he has discovered the means in the plays thought to be sequent to *Hamlet*—*Troilus and Cressida*, *Measure for Measure*, and *All's Well*—despite their flashes of poetry and constant assertion of the values of the popular dramatic tradition. Moral drama provides the needed pattern without pervasive indebtedness to neoclassic principles, stoicism, or the more theatrical conventions of coterie playwrights. Shakespeare, then, relaxes for the expansive canvas of *Antony and Cleopatra*, and in his last, dense tragedy *Coriolanus* writes something nearer than anything he has yet done to the tragedies of Chapman.

At any rate, the recrudescence of moral play structure in Shakespeare corresponds intriguingly to the Elizabethan twilight. In applying to Shakespearean tragedy his study of the dissolution of Elizabethan social structure, Paul Siegel argues that *Hamlet* dramatizes the struggle between acceptance of Christian humanist values and negativism within the breast of a perplexed protagonist. In *Othello*, *Macbeth*, and *Lear*, Siegel holds, the forces of cynicism are externally embodied in Shakespeare's villains.[18] Tempted, Othello and Macbeth choose the way of destruction, the murder of a good wife and Christian prince. Lear has already chosen to depose himself and, in folly, rewards the specious Goneril and Regan rather than the genuine Cordelia. Machiavellian values of an effete culture in England are given their day like the forces of Satan in the momentary triumph of evil characters over these deluded central figures and shown to be inadequate as guides to life. Against Iago and the Sisters Shakespeare's protagonists, like Mankynde himself, must oppose divided souls, and Lear cannot tell true from false for his pride. The structures of moral drama are it would seem perfectly suited to submitting the standards of the age to an ethical test.

But if we may, at the end of this long book, lift our eyes from the area of our specialty and crave the indulgence due to amateurs, we may I think perceive in Attic tragedy a precedent more satisfying ultimately than any explanation to be wrested from Shakespeare's England.[19] The recurrence of the designs of Mankynde's experience

midway in Shakespeare's career is, I have suggested, the same thing
as the occurrence there of Aristotelian plots leading into reversal and
realization. *Othello, Macbeth, King Lear*—these are his tragedies that
most resemble the *Oedipus* of Sophocles, and scholars of classical bent
have littered Shakespeare criticism with articles interpreting them
out of the *Poetics*. Why has this been possible?

In its Attic and Elizabethan manifestations alone did the art of
tragedy come about so to speak naturally, as against its artificial
rebirth in the work of a Milton or a Racine, and it passed through
a natural cycle in the productions of a number of closely contemporary
playwrights. Thus great tragedy as it first emerges exhibits a simple
grandeur of structure and implies unequivocal moral exhortation.
The typical theme is the just downfall of a wrongdoer (the early
Elizabethan theme), his end a spectacle of merited misfortune. This
begets awe at the terrible consequences of transgression, an emotion
opposite to Aristotle's pity. In its last phase great tragedy is typically
at the other extreme. The typical situation in Euripides or Webster
involves suffering women surrounded and persecuted by ruthless
men. And the heroines are more likely to be sinned against than
sinning. If they are not good, like Webster's Isabella, the Duchess of
Malfi, or the Troades, at least their immediate suffering, as with
Vittoria and Medea, seems disjunct from their defects of character.
Unmerited misfortune inspires pity. The didactic value of such
tragedy, if any, lies partly in skepticism and satire—upon war,
vanity, the courts of princes—but especially in stoicism, in a demonstration of *integer vitae* in a world which has become intolerable.
This tragic world is of course fearful, but the implicit moral exhortation is not to be afraid but to endure, not, as formerly, to
shun but to follow the example of the protagonist. Structurally, this
tragedy is likely to be episodic or scenic, ready to sacrifice the whole
to the momentary effect of the parts, inconsistent, improbable, its
mixture of diverse elements held in nervous combination. It slides
easily into melodrama. The poet is less likely to be priest or priest-
artist than artist in theatrical effects for their own sake.

Between, and briefly manifest midway in the career of the middle
dramatist, occurs the Aristotelian mean. The rare tragedies that

exempify it excite both fear and pity through the character of the protagonist, the one by our identification with him through his hamartia, the other by our perception of his good intentions. The didactic impulse, though felt to be present, is ultimately enigmatic. Not so much hero or universe is at fault as the irony of the combination. This, the drama suggests, is simply the human experience. The peripety and attendant realization that characterize the plot, no longer simple nor yet episodic, are the logical expression in the design of the flawed virtue of the protagonist acting in a world ambiguous to him. And he, spring of both the emotional and the structural complexity of the tragedy in which he figures, most fully reenacts the experience of the protagonist of preliterary ritual or primitive religious drama. The means of survival of the story of the Year-God in Greek tragedy, according to Gilbert Murray, "is that other persons and events are put into the forms that originally belonged to the Daimon."[20] Murray the Euripidean turns chiefly to Euripides and finds scattered remnants of the structure of the ritual. But the clearest reenactment of the story of the miraculous child who grows in beauty and strength, conquers, wins his bride, commits the sin of hybris or excess, and suffers defeat is the *Tyrannus*, the very inspiration of Aristotle's most stimulating ideas on the nature of tragedy. Something analogous happens with the similar forms of Mankynde's experience in Shakespeare, even though the sophisticated theology behind the Macro plays little resembles the prerational conception of general human experience embodied in the Greek ritual. Religious forms for a hero's experience, it may be, participate most intimately and fully at the center of the tragic cycle, and this is what we have found in Shakespeare.

What are we to think of a universe in which character and circumstance become so ironically interlocked as they do in *Oedipus*, and in *Othello*, *Macbeth*, and *King Lear*? The springs of tragic suffering still, in varying degrees, lie within. It is not imposed wholly from without as normally it is in Euripides and Webster. The tragic universe seems rational, but its justice is obscure and uninterpretable in contrast to that of the earliest great tragedy. The final chorus in the *Oedipus* suggests that such incertitude is typical of human experience. Despite the radical difference in his heritage, the words of Sophocles call to mind the conclusion of the model for the line of temptation plays that ends in Shakespeare: "Evyr at the begynnynge / Thynke on youre last endynge!" The mystery, in Shakespeare the Christian mystery of iniquity, has something to do with the full scope of human life, with the world and childhood, manhood, and old age. The world poses us a riddle, and the answer to the riddle is Mankind.

Notes

Chapter I

1. *Account Roll of the Priory of the Holy Trinity, Dublin, 1337–1346* (Dublin, 1891). Later editions by A. Brandl and O. Waterhouse are cited in Chapter V.

2. E E T S Extra Series 91. The introduction is by A. W. Pollard. There is a new edition for the E E T S by Mark Eccles, 1969. My citations are from this. Facsimiles of the MSS have been published by J. S. Farmer in his Tudor Facsimile Texts and by the Folger Shakespeare Library, where they reside.

3. The term *moralities* with the idea that the plays teach a "moral" may be traced back through Edmond Malone, Thomas Warton, and Bishop Thomas Percy to the Preface of Robert Dodsley's *Select Collection of Old Plays* (London, 1744), p. xiii. The terms fostered the universal Victorian contempt toward the theological drama as (Symonds) "an abortive side-effort" whose very name (Bates) "is like a yawn," and they continue to foster some modern confusions.

4. The opposite and still flourishing opinion is best represented by E. N. S. Thompson in his influential monograph "The English Moral Plays," *Transactions of the Connecticut Academy of Arts and Sciences*, 14 (1910), 291–413: "*The Castle of Perseverance*, it is clear, should not be considered primarily from the dramatic standpoint. Its influence on the growth of the English drama can not be disregarded, it is true, by the literary historian. But he who would appreciate the type of which *The Castle of Perseverance* is the truest representative, should remember that its author and its first audiences knew nothing of the drama *qua* drama, and should study it first, according to its intention, as a piece of didactic literature, *a sermo corporeus*" (p. 320). Richard Southern's study of the staging of the play, *The Medieval Theatre in the Round* (London, 1957), is alone sufficient to demolish this opinion.

5. Evolutionist assumptions underly all the best books on the subject, such as those of Chambers, Farnham, Rossiter, Craig, Spivack, Bevington, and Margeson cited in the bibliography. An interesting exposure of them in Chambers' *Mediaeval Stage* is the Introduction to O. B. Hardison, *Christian Rite and Christian Drama in the Middle Ages* (Baltimore,

1965). For a deadly definition consider W. R. Mackenzie, *The English Moralities from the Point of View of Allegory* (Boston and London, 1914), pp. 8–9: "A Morality is a play, allegorical in structure, which has for its main object the teaching of some lesson for the guidance of life, and in which the principal characters are personified abstractions or highly universalized types." This persists, A. P. Rossiter, for example, hampering himself with it at the start of his chapter on "The Morality Genus," *English Drama from Early Times to the Elizabethans* (London, 1950), p. 95. By "classifications" I mean particularly what seems to me the barren scientism of R. L. Ramsay's Introduction to his edition of Skelton's *Magnyfycence,* E E T S Extra Series 98 (London, 1906), pp. ix–cxiv. Ramsay analyzes plays into various plot motives (the Coming of Death, the Debate of the Daughters of God, the Conflict of Virtues and Vices, etc.) so that a given play becomes a conglomeration of some of these, not something designed as a whole. Seen as entities, English moral plays work out either the temptation or the death of their central figure.

6. *English Religious Drama* (Oxford, 1955), p. 383.

7. Ibid., p. 384, where Craig, however, ventures to add that the old conflict now internalized "is perhaps not absent from *Othello* and *Macbeth.*"

8. *The Mediaeval Stage* (Oxford, 1903), II, 156.

Chapter II

1. The account is by R. Willis, *Mount Tabor, or Private Exercises of a Penitent Sinner* (London, 1639), pp. 110–14. Often reprinted, it may be read in Bevington, *From Mankind to Marlowe* (Cambridge, Mass., 1962), pp. 13–14.

2. The accompanying chart lists the relevant Tudor plays, distinguished by their preservation of all or a significant part of the design of Mankynde's experience, in relation to their theological prototypes and to the Shakespearean counterparts of these.

Early Tudor is distinguished from Elizabethan on the basis of probable time of composition, not date of printing. *Everyman* is placed in brackets because it may not be part of the English development of moral drama, Lyndsay's *Satyre* because it is Scottish, and the Digby *Marie Magdalene* because it poses unsolved problems making it difficult to date (1480–1520?) and even to account for. *The Cradle of Security*, the sole Tudor play on record that may have derived from the coming of death, is not extant.

Classes of Plot

	Full Scope	Temptation	Coming of Death
			The Pride of Life
PRE-TUDOR	*The Castell of Perseverance* ————————————		
		Wisdom	
		Mankind	[*Everyman*]
EARLY TUDOR	*Nature*	*Magnyfycence*	
	Nature of the Four Elementes	*Godly Queene Hester*	
		Kyng Johan	
	Worlde and the Chylde	[*Ane Satyre*]	
	Wyt and Science	*Lusty Juventus*	
	Impaciente Poverte	[*Marie Magdalene (Digby)*]	
		Marie Magdalene	
		Calisto and Melebea	
		Welth and Helth	
		Respublica	
ELIZA-BETHAN	*The Longer Thou Livest*	*Pacient Grissell*	
		Horestes	
		Inough is as Good	
		Cambises	(*The Cradle of Security*)
		Apius and Virginia	
		The Conflict of Conscience	
SHAKE-SPEAREAN		*Othello*	
		Macbeth	*King Lear*

3. *Magnyfycence*, ed. R. L. Ramsay, E E T S (London, 1906), p. 58.

4. *Wit and Science*, ed. A. Brown, W. W. Greg, F. P. Wilson, Malone Society Reprints (1951), ll. 828ff.

5. Ed. A. Brandl, *Quellen des Weltlichen Dramas in England* (Strassburg, 1898), p. 146. This is the second of two realizations in the doubled play. The first, p. 114, is apparently spontaneous.

6. R. Wever, *Lusty Juventus*, ed. J. S. Farmer, Tudor Facsimile Texts (1905), $E_{iii}r$. The actual tempter was Hypocrisy.

7. *Ane Satyre of the Thrie Estaits*, ed. James Kinsley (London, 1954), pp. 104ff. Part I of the *Satyre* is the temptation play.

8. *Calisto and Melebea*, ed. W. W. Greg, Malone Society Reprints (1908), ll. 930ff.

9. Ed. F. I. Carpenter (Chicago, 1904), ll. 1027–1454. The temptation plot concludes when Christ raises the contrite Marie, and the remainder of the play dramatizes Luke.

10. *Godly Queene Hester*, ed. W. W. Greg in Bang's *Materialien*, V (Louvain, 1904), ll. 971–74.

11. Mark Eccles, ed., *The Macro Plays*, E E T S (London, 1969).

12. Only this tempter, called Titivillus, among the characters in *Mankind* possibly partakes of the supernatural. He can make himself invisible. He is usually taken to be a devil, or the Devil, but if so he is by far a more humanized version of the Devil than was the Lucifer in *Wisdom*. Lucifer's motive, we recall, was envy of man for having received his lost heavenly place in the scheme of things, a motive replaceable by human equivalents but not itself translatable to any human being. Titivillus never calls himself a devil, nor do his cronies, and his motive for disgracing Mankynde is explicitly to "venge" the beating that Mankynde gave them in the opening phase of the plot. He also exhibits an interest in money, partly but not entirely extra-dramatic. The rogue-actors advertising the entrance of Titivillus before collecting money from the audience call him a man: "We intende to gather mony, yf yt plesse yowr neclygence, / For a man wyth a hede that ys. of grett omnipotens" (ll. 460–61). And again (l. 463), "He ys a worschyppull man, sers,"—one who loves not groats, pence, or twopence. No, "Gyf ws rede reyallys, yf ye wyll se hys abhomynabull presens." As Titivillus makes his way to the stage, Nowadays cries, "he ys a goodly man, sers; make space and be ware!" The editors Pollard and Furnivall assume that the abominable presence is that of a devil, and it may be so, but beyond his talent for invisibility there is no evidence for this conclusion until Mercy's interpretation of Mankynde's experience at the end of the play. Mercy declares (l. 886): "And propyrly Titivillus syngnyfyth the Fend of helle." But the line just before this one explains that New Guise, Nowadays, and Nought "the World we may hem call," and so the passage appears to involve a measure of schematic interpretation after the fact, an effort to fit the characters into the scheme of World, Devil, and Flesh (Mankynde's own unclean body), no longer present themselves as participants as they were in the *Castell* play. Titivillus may be said to stand for the Devil in the way that the other rogues represent the world. The force of "properly" and "signifies" is not that he *is* Satan but that for practical purposes he is equivalent in Mankynde's life to Satan. He is, precisely, a demi-devil, and this tempter who

is partly a man, who wants to get back at the protagonist for an injury to his friends, who explains his clever strategy to the audience like Lucifer before him, and moreover who for the first time among tempters in the moral drama proceeds partly by slandering the play's one wholly good character, surely ought to be included along with the Vices of later plays in the family of Iago.

13. Ed. W. W. Greg, Malone Society Reprints (1910).

14. Although Phillip introduces a tempter independently of the versions of the story already mentioned, it is worth noting that William Forrest's *History of Grisild the Second*, a book-length poem in rhyme royal addressed to Queen Mary and explicitly related to Henry VIII's treatment of her mother Catherine, makes it be at the instigation of the Devil that "*Walter* sought meanys to bee dyvorsed from Grisilde," as the title of Ch. 5 phrases the idea. The first stanza in this chapter declares that after twenty years of marriage,

> The cursed Enemye, sower of dyscorde,
> Began to sue his accustomed trace,
> Goode *Grysildis* estate for to difface,
> Moste wickedlye that anye can discusse;
> All, for she was to hym contraryous.

Under Elizabeth, Phillip probably did not wish to retain the political application given the tale by Forrest, though we may recall that *Godly Queene Hester*, almost certainly an allegory of Henry and Catherine, was seen fit to be printed in 1561. It may still have been Forrest who gave Phillip the hint for casting the Vice of Heywood perhaps for the first time in the Devil's part.

15. *The Medieval Heritage of Elizabethan Tragedy* (Berkeley, 1936), p. 250.

16. Henry E. Huntington Facsimile Reprints, II (1920), introductory note by Seymour De Ricci.

17. In the first phase of the action, before Worldly Man turns tyrant, the virtue Contentation remarks that of late days Ambition corrupted the realm, reigning in those who should rather be examples to others:

> the Breethern they did disdain,
> And burned with fire, the Childe with the mother.
> It is often seen that such monstrous Ambition,
> As spareth not to spil the blood of the innocent
> Wil not greatly stick to fall to sedition.   ($B_{ii}v$)

The reference is to the cruelty of ministers under Queen Mary, notably Reginal Pole, who had advanced themselves politically through persecution of Protestants. Women were burned on several occasions in 1555 and 1556, and in 1557 a mother gave birth to her infant in the flames. Wager is also distressed by the greed of magistrates now in the first years of Elizabethan Protestantism and their parsimony toward the Genevan wing of the church. Just as the protagonist is about to make his decision in the temptation scene, the virtuous man Inough cites those Protestants deprived of wealth under Mary who swore that when God again restored his verity and sent his word again they would renounce the way of covetousness. Now, however, these same men make laws in the name of covetousness, buy and sell leases and benefices, double the price of wares. What is more,

> So shamefully Gods ministers they poule & shave:
> That not half inough to live upon they have.
> But it is an olde saying and a true certainly:
> It wil not out of the flesh that is bred in the bone verily.
> The worldly man wil needs be a worldly man stil:
>
> $(D_{iv}v)$

Chapter III

1. Ed. Mark Eccles, *The Macro Plays*, E E T S (London, 1969).

2. Willard Farnham, *Shakespeare's Tragic Frontier* (Berkeley and Los Angeles, 1950), p. 79.

3. Cf. Sir Arthur Quiller-Couch, *Shakespeare's Workmanship* (London, 1918), pp. 1–53.

4. *The Medieval Theatre in the Round* (London, 1957), p. 174.

5. *Shakespeare's Imagery* (Boston, 1958), pp. 324–27. Originally published 1935.

6. In *The Well Wrought Urn* (New York, 1947), pp. 21–46.

7. Eccles prints as one word, Alholy, taking "holy" to mean "wholly." So had Furnivall, followed by Southern in his paraphrase. The reading seems to me to lack point.

8. *Prudentius*, ed. with an English translation by H. J. Thomson (Cambridge, Mass., 1949), p. 317.

9. The military siege of the Castle offers the nearest approach in extant moral drama to *Les Gieux des sept vertuz e des sept pechiez mortelz*, played at Tours in 1390, and to the Paternoster plays of England. These brought the conception of the military psychomachia to the threshold of English drama but, presumably lacking Mankynde, were not true plays. On this point see Hardin Craig, *English Religious Drama* (Oxford, 1955), pp. 337–41.

10. *The Medieval Theatre in the Round*, p. 199.
11. Ibid., p. 208.
12. See ibid., pp. 7–8, 209; *Macro Plays*, p. 2.

Chapter IV

1. Ed. Mark Eccles, *The Macro Plays*, E E T S (London, 1969).

2. On stage tradition, see Marvin Rosenberg, *The Masks of Othello* (Berkeley, 1961), p. 230. On the portrait contemporary with *Othello* see Bernard Harris, "A Portrait of a Moor," *Shakespeare Survey*, 11 (1958), 89–97.

3. Iago is not, as Bernard Spivack has tried to show in a study from which in other respects I have derived great aid and comfort, a demi-Vice out of Tudor drama. He is rather what Othello is at last given the insight to call him, a "demy-Divell." See Spivack's *Shakespeare and the Allegory of Evil* (New York, 1958), pp. 52, 132–33, et passim. Cf. Leah Scragg, "Iago—Vice or Devil?" *Shakespeare Survey*, 21 (1968), 53–65, and Robert H. West, *Shakespeare and the Outer Mystery* (Lexington, Ky., 1968), Ch. VII.

The evidence of role joins with that of diabolic allusiveness. Mankynde's tempter in the next and last religious drama of temptation, *Mankind*. "syngnyfyth the Fend of helle" (l. 886), that is, stands for Satan. Not so much his motive to "venge" a wrong as his use for the first time of slander to alienate the protagonist from the single embodiment of goodness in his life aligns him, along with Lucifer in *Wisdom*, with Iago. In early Tudor plays, it is true, the tempter is never the Devil, but neither is he usually the Vice. He is a figure lacking the distinct qualities of the Vice—Aman, Celestina, Sedicyon alias Stevyn Langton—while the Vice appears in the interludes of John Heywood without reference to religious drama. The Vice may play a tempter, chiefly in early Elizabethan hybrid plays, but retains (notably Politic Perswasion in *Patient Grissell*) a Heywoodian zaniness that Iago does not. Spivack proves that Iago owes much to the Vice of intermediate drama, but the distinctive allusiveness of Shakespeare's arch tempter is to the Devil, and this is not I think, pace Spivack, "too much a moral cliché to be enlightening." Spivack's preoccupation with the Vice, and his evolutionist's assumptions, cause him to dismiss Iago's obviously Luciferian quality and to relegate *Wisdom* to an unimportant place in the background of *Othello*. The other figures in mature drama whom Spivack derives from the Vice do not approach Iago's degree of this quality. None—not Barabas, Hoffman, Richard III, Don John, Lorenzo in *The First Part of Jeronimo*, Roderick in *The Trial of Chivalry*—plays in relationship to a central figure the role Lucifer played against Mankynde. Chronology, no more than the evidence of role, will support the neat hypothesis of Spivack that the Vice condenses the many vices in plays like *The Castell of Perseverance.* See L. W. Cushman, *The Devil and the Vice in the English Dramatic Literature before Shakespeare* (Halle, 1900), p. 63; E. K. Chambers, *The Mediaeval Stage* (Oxford, 1903), II, 203–5; F. W. Mares, "The Origin of the Figure called 'the Vice' in Tudor Drama," *HLQ*, 22 (1958), 11–29. The name of the Vice may be otherwise explained, and he himself is not best regarded as a product of the psychomachia at all but as a free-lance character from outside the drama as we know it who plays many parts in Tudor drama including that of the Fiend while never becoming so fiendish as Iago. We need only free ourselves from evolutionist prejudices to perceive this.

4. *Ancient Mysteries from the Digby Manuscripts* (London, 1835), pp. xxxii ff. Quoted by Pollard, *Macro Plays*, p. xxii.

5. For l. 378 I adopt the Digby reading "prove" for Macro "provyt," which looks like a scribal anticipation of "yt" and damages the parallelism of the sentence.

6. Walter K. Smart, *Some English and Latin Sources and Parallels for the Morality of Wisdom* (Menasha, Wis., 1912).

7. "The *Othello* Music," *The Wheel of Fire* (New York, 1957), pp. 97–119. Originally pubished 1930.

8. To this extent I disagree with Paul N. Siegel, "The Damnation of Othello," *PMLA*, 68 (1953), 1068–78, revised as Ch. VI of *Shakespearean Tragedy and the Elizabethan Compromise* (New York, 1957). Cf. West, *Shakespeare and the Outer Mystery*, Ch. VIII.

Chapter V

1. This form of theater is most extensively studied, though from the *Castell* MS, not that of *The Pride of Life*, by Richard Southern, *The Medieval Theatre in the Round* (London, 1957).

2. Ed. Mills, *Account Roll of the Priory of the Holy Trinity, Dublin* (Dublin, 1891). Ed. A. Brandl, *Quellen des Weltlichen Dramas in England* (Strassburg, 1898), with a translation into German. Ed. O. Waterhouse, *The Non-Cycle Mystery Plays*, E E T S Extra Series 104 (London, 1909). I have used Brandl's text with a very few modifications from that of Waterhouse.

3. *Plays of Our Forefathers* (New York, 1907), pp. 293–94.

4. *A Select Collection of Old Plays* (London, 1744), p. xiii.

5. *ELH*, 15 (1948), 93–109.

6. "Man darf ihn eher mit den Hofnarren in Beziehung setzen, die im XV. Jahrhundert in England beliebt wurden." *Quellen*, p. xv.

7. See F. H. Mares, "The Origin of the Figure called 'the Vice' in Tudor Drama," *HLQ*, 22 (1958), 11–29.

8. The Coventry Herod, *Two Coventry Corpus Christi Plays*, ed. H. Craig, E E T S Extra Series 87 (London, 1902), p. 19, ll. 537–39, also rests while his Nuntius is on an errand. Cf. Herod Antipas, *Ludus Coventriae*, p. 273, ll. 66–69.

9. Ed. W. W. Greg in Bang's *Materialien zur Kunde*, IV and XXIV (Louvain, 1904 and 1909). The two editions by John Scot. I have used Greg 1904.

10. *Everyman: A Comparative Study of Texts and Sources* (Louvain, 147), p. 179. Vol. 20 of Materials for the Study of Old English Drama.

11. Ed. Mark Eccles, *The Macro Plays*, E E T S (London, 1969).

12. Ed. W. Linow, *Erlanger Beiträge*, I (Erlangen, 1889), 28.

13. Ed. K. Brunner, "Mittelenglische Todesgeschichte," *Archiv für das Studium der neueren Sprachen*, 167 (1935), 23.

14. *The Medieval Heritage of Elizabethan Tragedy* (Berkeley, 1936), p. 452.

15. I owe this term to an excellent study of the ending of the play by J. Stampfer, "The Catharsis of *King Lear*," *Shakespeare Survey*, 13 (1960), 1–10.

Chapter VI

1. *Endeavors of Art: A Study of Form in Elizabethan Drama* (Madison, Wis., 1954), p. 145. Adams, *English Domestic, or, Homiletic Tragedy* (New York, 1943), Ch. IV, VI. Harbage, *Shakespeare's Audience* (New York, 1941), Ch. III.

2. *English Religious Drama* (Oxford, 1955), p. 383.

3. The important study of these "morals" is Louis B. Wright, "Social Aspects of Some Belated Moralities," *Anglia*, 54 (1930), 107–48. Cf. John W. McCutchan, "Personified Abstractions as Characters in Elizabethan Drama," Univ. of Virginia *Abstracts of Dissertations* (1949), pp. 11–14; E. N. S. Thompson, *Literary Bypaths of the Renaissance* (New Haven, 1924). Yet one strange moral, *If it be not Good, the Divel is in it*, demonstrates that the temptation plot could reassert itself in such surroundings. It reflects the same social conditions as the plays from the last decade of Elizabeth's reign just considered, though Chambers (III, 297) accepts a date of 1610–1612. The text, dated 1612, calls it "A New Play, AS IT HATH BIN lately Acted, with great applause, by the Queenes

Majesties Servants: At the Red Bull. Written by Thomas Dekker." Like the plays just listed, this concerns itself with corruption and injustice in several orders of the realm, here nominally Naples. The noble, clerical, and mercantile estates fall from virtue through temptation by three devils sent from Hell. The result of a complex merging of three parallel lines of plot is that the moral awakening of King Alphonso counts for Naples generally. He becomes a Mankynde-figure like Assuerus whose cardinal virtue is justice, and the predominant Alphonso plot, although the fact is greatly obscured by the threads of intrigue, is a reenactment in the Jacobean theater of the temptation plot in its early Tudor, nontragic form. Distinctly "not Good," the piece clarifies the distinction between an odd throwback to an old form and the artistic apotheosis of it in Shakespeare.

4. Thus Willard Thorp, *The Triumph of Realism in Elizabethan Drama 1558–1612* (Princeton, 1928), p. 48: "*Faustus* stands at the end of a tradition. Through it a host of inglorious Woodeses and Wagers speak their hearts." Cf. Craig, *English Religious Drama*, pp. 386–89.

5. W. W. Greg, ed., *Marlowe's Doctor Faustus, 1604–1616* (Oxford, 1950). My references, except for the one noted, are to the B text of 1616.

6. *From Mankind to Marlowe* (Cambridge, Mass., 1962), pp. 252–58.

7. Reprinted by H. Logeman as *The English Faust-Book of 1592* (Ghent and Amsterdam, 1900), and by Basil Ashmore, ed., *The Tragical History of Doctor Faustus* (London, 1948), pp. 103–215.

8. Greg, p. 102. Greg, p. 103, adds that the direction "Thunder. Enter Lucifer and 4 devils, Faustus to them with this speech," B, ll. 255–56, was added "not, as might at first appear, to theatrical effect, but to an altered conception of the hero's downfall."

9. Greg, p. 131.

10. Rossiter, ed., *Woodstock, a Moral History* (London, 1946), p. 7. Cf. Sir Arthur Quiller-Couch, *Shakespeare's Workmanship* (London, 1918), p. 115; John Dover Wilson, *The Fortunes of Falstaff* (Cambridge, 1945), pp. 20ff.

1. *From Mankind to Marlowe*, p. 185.

12. I shall later quote from my own edition, in *Tudor Plays* (Garden City, N.Y., 1966). The play was first edited by F. S. Boas and A. W. Reed (Oxford, 1926).

13. Ed. A. Brandl, *Quellen des Weltlichen Dramas in England vor Shakespeare* (Strassburg, 1898).

14. *Shakespeare and the Allegory of Evil*, p. 87.

15. Ibid., p. 88.

16. "The Salvation of Lear," *ELH*, 15 (1948), 93–109.

17. *Shakespeare and the Rival Traditions* (New York, 1952), pp. 295 et passim.

18. *Shakespearean Tragedy and the Elizabethan Compromise* (New York, 1957), pp. 86–87 et passim. Irving Ribner, *Patterns in Shakespearian Tragedy* (London, 1960), develops a similar notion of Shakespeare's cultural role to that of Harbage and Siegel. He remarks in passing that Macbeth, p. 160, is "in the position of the traditional morality-play hero," that, p. 102, the temptation scene in *Othello* "is cast in the traditional pattern of the morality drama." He cites with approval, p. 117, Campbell's article (see n. 16 above) connecting Lear and Everyman.

19. My ideas about Sophocles and Euripides set forth on the following pages were inspired by the discussions of these playwrights in H. D. F. Kitto, *Greek Tragedy, A Literary Study* (London, 1939).

20. See "Excursus on the Ritual Forms Preserved in Greek Tragedy," in Jane Ellen Harrison's *Themis* (Cambridge, 1912), pp. 341–63. I am indebted to the comment on Murray's study in Francis Fergusson, *The Idea of a Theatre* (Princeton, 1949), p. 33.

List of Authorities

The Most Useful Studies Bearing in Various Ways upon Shakespeare's Relationship to the Interludes and to the Theological Dramas Preceding Them

Adams, Henry Hitch. *English Domestic, or, Homiletic Tragedy, being an account of the Development of the Tragedy of the Common Man.* New York, 1943.

Baskervill, C. R. *English Elements in Jonson's Early Comedy.* Univ. of Texas *Bulletin*, No. 178 (1911).

Bethell, Samuel L. *Shakespeare and the Popular Dramatic Tradition.* Durham, N.C., 1944.

Bevington, David M. *From Mankind to Marlowe.* Cambridge, Mass., 1962.

Campbell, Oscar J. "The Salvation of Lear." *ELH*, 15 (1948), 93–109.

Chambers, E. K. *The Elizabethan Stage.* 4 vols. Oxford, 1923.

——. *The Mediaeval Stage.* 2 vols. Oxford, 1903.

——. *William Shakespeare, a Study of Facts and Problems.* 2 vols. Oxford, 1930.

Craig, Hardin. *English Religious Drama of the Middle Ages.* Oxford, 1955.

——. "Morality Plays and Elizabethan Drama." *ShQ*, 1 (1950), 64–72.

Crosse, Gordon. *The Religious Drama.* London, 1913.

Cushman, L. W. *The Devil and the Vice in the English Dramatic Literature before Shakespeare.* Halle, 1900.

Farnham, Willard. *The Medieval Heritage of Elizabethan Tragedy.* Berkeley, 1936.

Gatch, Katherine. "Shakespeare's Allusions to the Older Drama." *PQ*, 7 (1928), 27–44.

Greg, W. W. *A Bibliography of English Printed Drama to the Restoration.* Vol. I (to 1616). London, 1939.

Harbage, Alfred. *Annals of English Drama, 975–1700.* Philadelphia and London, 1940. Revised by S. Schoenbaum, London, 1964.

——. *Shakespeare and the Rival Traditions.* New York, 1952.

Hunter, E. R. "*Macbeth* as a Morality." Shakespeare Association *Bulletin*, 7 (1937), 217–35.

Margeson, J. M. *The Origins of English Tragedy.* Oxford, 1967.

Ribner, Irving. "Morality Roots of the Tudor History Play." *Tulane Studies in English*, 4 (1954), 21–43.

Rossiter, A. P. *English Drama from Early Times to the Elizabethans: Its Background, Origins, and Developments.* London, 1950.

Scragg, Leah. "Iago—Vice or Devil?" *Shakespeare Survey*, 21 (1968), 53–65.

Siegel, Paul N. *Shakespearean Tragedy and the Elizabethan Compromise.* New York, 1957.

Southern, Richard. *The Medieval Theatre in the Round.* London, 1957.

Spivack, Bernard. *Shakespeare and the Allegory of Evil.* New York, 1958.

Taylor, George C. "The Medieval Element in Shakespeare." Shakespeare Association *Bulletin*, 7 (1937), 208–16. Bibliography of studies published before Farnham's *Medieval Heritage*.

Thorp, Willard. *The Triumph of Realism in Elizabethan Drama 1558–1612.* Princeton, 1928.

West, Robert H. *Shakespeare and the Outer Mystery.* Lexington, Ky., 1968.

Wickham, Glynne W. *Shakespeare's Dramatic Heritage.* New York, 1969.

Wilson, John Dover. *The Fortunes of Falstaff.* Cambridge, 1945.

Index